T0209455

An Analysis of

Walter Benjamin's

The Work of Art in the Age of Mechanical Reproduction

Rachele Dini

Published by Macat International Ltd
24:13 Coda Centre, 189 Munster Road, London SW6 6AW.

Distributed exclusively by Routledge
2 Park Square, Milton Park, Abingdon, Oxon OX14 4RN
711 Third Avenue, New York, NY 10017, USA

Routledge is an imprint of the Taylor & Francis Group, an informa business

www.macat.com
info@macat.com

Cataloguing in Publication Data
A catalogue record for this book is available from the British Library.
Library of Congress Cataloguing-in-Publication Data is available upon request.
Cover illustration: David Newton

ISBN 978-1-912304-04-2 (hardback)
ISBN 978-1-912284-75-7 (paperback)
ISBN 978-1-912284-89-4 (e-book)

Notice
The information in this book is designed to orientate readers of the work under analysis,
to elucidate and contextualise its key ideas and themes, and to aid in the development
of critical thinking skills. It is not meant to be used, nor should it be used, as a
substitute for original thinking or in place of original writing or research. References and
notes are provided for informational purposes and their presence does not constitute
endorsement of the information or opinions therein. This book is presented solely for
educational purposes. It is sold on the understanding that the publisher is not engaged
to provide any scholarly advice. The publisher has made every effort to ensure that
this book is accurate and up-to-date, but makes no warranties or representations with
regard to the completeness or reliability of the information it contains. The information
and the opinions provided herein are not guaranteed or warranted to produce particular
results and may not be suitable for students of every ability. The publisher shall not be
liable for any loss, damage or disruption arising from any errors or omissions, or from
the use of this book, including, but not limited to, special, incidental, consequential or
other damages caused, or alleged to have been caused, directly or indirectly, by the
information contained within.

CONTENTS

THE MACAT LIBRARY

The Macat Library is a series of unique academic explorations of seminal works in the humanities and social sciences – books and papers that have had a significant and widely recognised impact on their disciplines. It has been created to serve as much more than just a summary of what lies between the covers of a great book. It illuminates and explores the influences on, ideas of, and impact of that book. Our goal is to offer a learning resource that encourages critical thinking and fosters a better, deeper understanding of important ideas.

Each publication is divided into three Sections: Influences, Ideas, and Impact. Each Section has four Modules. These explore every important facet of the work, and the responses to it.

This Section-Module structure makes a Macat Library book easy to use, but it has another important feature. Because each Macat book is written to the same format, it is possible (and encouraged!) to cross-reference multiple Macat books along the same lines of inquiry or research. This allows the reader to open up interesting interdisciplinary pathways.

To further aid your reading, lists of glossary terms and people mentioned are included at the end of this book (these are indicated by an asterisk [*] throughout) – as well as a list of works cited.

Macat has worked with the University of Cambridge to identify the elements of critical thinking and understand the ways in which six different skills combine to enable effective thinking.
Three allow us to fully understand a problem; three more give us the tools to solve it. Together, these six skills make up the **PACIER** model of critical thinking. They are:

ANALYSIS – understanding how an argument is built
EVALUATION – exploring the strengths and weaknesses of an argument
INTERPRETATION – understanding issues of meaning

CREATIVE THINKING – coming up with new ideas and fresh connections
PROBLEM-SOLVING – producing strong solutions
REASONING – creating strong arguments

To find out more, visit **WWW.MACAT.COM.**

CRITICAL THINKING AND "THE WORK OF ART IN THE AGE OF MECHANICAL REPRODUCTION"

Primary critical thinking skill: CREATIVE THINKING
Secondary critical thinking skill: INTERPRETATION

Walter Benjamin is a prime example of a creative thinker. In "The Work of Art in the Age of Mechanical Reproduction," he sets out a series of seemingly unrelated phenomena—the possibilities opened up by the advent of film and photography, fascism's reliance on spectacle, and art and literature's anticipation of new technologies—and connects them in new ways to propose a novel theory of art criticism. The fourteen strands of Benjamin's thesis, and the surprising conclusions he draws in his epilogue, do not progress in a linear way and the essay itself is impossible to classify. This is art criticism, but not like that proposed by his contemporaries, whom he explicitly says are outdated. Rather, "The Work of Art in the Age of Mechanical Reproduction" is a critique of fascism's adoption of the new media developed under capitalism. Benjamin takes issue with his fellow Marxists' critiques of mass culture, since he actually thinks that by watching movies, people can learn to be *more* skeptical and critical of propaganda. His thinking, alas, relies on poetic language and imagery, florid turns of phrase, and startling analogies that would leave some philosophers puzzled.

"The Work of Art" is an example of Benjamin's "constellatory thinking"—a term he used to describe his tendency to produce a cluster of ideas rather than one final statement. The fact that Benjamin aspired to one day write a book entirely composed of fragments of quotations reflects this same approach. This thinking imitates the fragmentary, experimental approach of the artists he most admired—but it is a far cry from the academic writing of his contemporaries or, indeed, of today.

ABOUT THE AUTHOR OF THE ORIGINAL WORK

Walter Benjamin (1892–1940) was a leftist German Jewish cultural critic and essayist best known for "The Work of Art in the Age of Mechanical Reproduction," "Theses on the Philosophy of History," and his unfinished book, *The Arcades Project*. Benjamin is associated with the "Frankfurt School"—a group of scholars based at the Institute for Social Research at the University of Frankfurt. Like Benjamin, these scholars were concerned with the relationship between cultural production, capitalism, and society, and were actively engaged in opposing the rise of fascism. Difficult to categorize within any one discipline, and used by scholars in areas as various as art history, literary studies, media studies, and history, Benjamin's work probes the political ramifications of the transformation of art and its reception following the advent of photography and film. Unrecognized during his lifetime, and largely forgotten in the decades following his suspected suicide while fleeing the Gestapo, Benjamin is now recognized as a critical theorist and cultural studies scholar who was ahead of his time.

ABOUT THE AUTHOR OF THE ANALYSIS

Rachele Dini is a lecturer in English literature at the University of Roehampton. Her areas of specialty include literary avant-gardes, Marxist literary criticism, and discard studies. Her first book, *Consumerism, Waste and Re-use in Twentieth-Century Fiction: Legacies of the Avant-Garde*, was published by Palgrave Macmillan in 2016. She received her undergraduate degree from the University of Cambridge, her MA from King's College, London, and her PhD from UCL.

ABOUT MACAT

GREAT WORKS FOR CRITICAL THINKING

Macat is focused on making the ideas of the world's great thinkers accessible and comprehensible to everybody, everywhere, in ways that promote the development of enhanced critical thinking skills.

It works with leading academics from the world's top universities to produce new analyses that focus on the ideas and the impact of the most influential works ever written across a wide variety of academic disciplines. Each of the works that sit at the heart of its growing library is an enduring example of great thinking. But by setting them in context – and looking at the influences that shaped their authors, as well as the responses they provoked – Macat encourages readers to look at these classics and game-changers with fresh eyes. Readers learn to think, engage and challenge their ideas, rather than simply accepting them.

'Macat offers an amazing first-of-its-kind tool for interdisciplinary learning and research. Its focus on works that transformed their disciplines and its rigorous approach, drawing on the world's leading experts and educational institutions, opens up a world-class education to anyone.'

Andreas Schleicher
Director for Education and Skills, Organisation for Economic
Co-operation and Development

'Macat is taking on some of the major challenges in university education … They have drawn together a strong team of active academics who are producing teaching materials that are novel in the breadth of their approach.'

Prof Lord Broers,
former Vice-Chancellor of the University of Cambridge

'The Macat vision is exceptionally exciting. It focuses upon new modes of learning which analyse and explain seminal texts which have profoundly influenced world thinking and so social and economic development. It promotes the kind of critical thinking which is essential for any society and economy. This is the learning of the future.'

Rt Hon Charles Clarke, former UK Secretary of State for Education

'The Macat analyses provide immediate access to the critical conversation surrounding the books that have shaped their respective discipline, which will make them an invaluable resource to all of those, students and teachers, working in the field.'

Professor William Tronzo, University of California at San Diego

WAYS IN TO THE TEXT

KEY POINTS

- Walter Benjamin was a leftist German Jewish philosopher best known for "The Work of Art in the Age of Mechanical Reproduction"[1] and "Theses on the Philosophy of History."[2]
- "The Work of Art" examines the relationship between art, innovations in the technologies used to make art, and politics.
- The essay anticipated post-World War II* academic discussions concerning new media, culture, and politics.

Who Was Walter Benjamin?

Walter Benjamin was a German Jewish philosopher whose writings on capitalism's effects on art, politics, and social life remain vitally important today. Benjamin was born in Berlin in 1892 to an affluent household, but experienced poverty and hardship throughout much of his adult life. His early thought was influenced by the educational reformer Gustav Wyneken, whom he met while a student at one of Wyneken's boarding schools. Wyneken was the editor of a radical* youth journal, *Der Anfang* (German for "The Beginning"), which was the voice of an intellectual youth movement devoted to the ideals of eighteenth- and nineteenth-century German philosophers, such as Hegel, Goethe, Kant, and Nietzsche.

Benjamin studied philosophy at the Universities of Freiburg, Berlin, Munich, and latterly Bern, where he received his PhD in 1919. While in Munich, he met the philosopher Gershom Scholem,* who became a lifelong friend, and who introduced him to Jewish mysticism.* His intellectual career took off in 1923, however, with the founding of the Institute for Social Research, where he met the philosophers Theodor Adorno* and Georg Lukács,* whose works (particularly Lukács's 1920 book, *Theory of the Novel*) profoundly influenced his writing.

Benjamin wrote the first version of "The Work of Art" towards the end of 1935 while living in Paris, where he had been forced to move after the Nazis came to power and took away his German citizenship. A modified translation was published in French by the Institute for Social Research,* a hub for Marxist scholars that had moved from the University of Frankfurt to New York City due to fear of Nazi persecution. In an effort not to alienate a more pro-capitalist US audience, the editors omitted references to Karl Marx.* The version most frequently read today is the one Benjamin re-wrote in 1939, just as Europe was about to be torn apart by World War II and barely a year before Benjamin's suspected suicide while fleeing the Gestapo.* This version was not published in English until 1968.

What Does "The Work of Art" Say?
In "The Work of Art," Walter Benjamin argues that the concepts emphasized by traditional art criticism,* such as "creativity and genius, eternal value and mystery," are outdated. This is owing to two things: the emergence of new art forms, such as photography and film, which are viewed collectively and are experienced by the individual in different ways from painting or theatre; and the rise of fascism* across Europe, which relied on manipulating theatrical and artistic rhetoric to influence public opinion.

For Benjamin, an audience accustomed to film will be less likely to be taken in by the spectacular displays used by fascist leaders to manipulate their opinions and draw attention away from social inequality. Film is a counter to what he calls the "aestheticization of politics,"* because it encourages distraction, which can be used in turn to ignore propaganda. Benjamin proposes a series of alternative concepts through which to understand art's reception in the age of these new technologies, and through which to identify art's revolutionary potential. The concepts he advances "differ from the more familiar terms [of art theory] in that they are completely useless for the purposes of fascism. They are, on the other hand, useful for the formulation of revolutionary demands in the politics of art."

For the fascists, Benjamin argues, audience reception of an artwork is fixed regardless of the place or time period in which it is viewed: thus, its value and meaning become unchangeable. Communists instead consider the network of forces at play in the social, cultural, and political conditions in which the artwork was produced, and they understand that an artwork's meaning and its reception changes in and through time, so that even its own past is subject to re-interpretation. For Benjamin, the work of art in the age of mechanical reproduction reveals how the past can be shaped in new ways by the present: film, for example, reconfigures the meaning of Shakespeare's plays in new ways that have an impact on the fixed words of the text. If the past is fluid, then so is the present. This in turn means that change is possible: Benjamin argues that we can transform the ways in which technology is organized, not only to produce art, but to oppose oppressive regimes.

While Benjamin's essay did not have much influence during his lifetime or during the first decades following its initial publication, it has had an enormous influence on art criticism, cultural studies, and literary theory since the late 1960s. The ideas set out in "The Work of Art" underpin John Berger's* influential work of art criticism, *Ways of Seeing* (1977), Susan Sontag's* study, *On Photography* (1977), and a wealth of literary and art criticism on twentieth-century literature and art as they relate to politics and technology. More recently, Benjamin's work has been mentioned alongside that of his fellow philosophers and friends Theodor Adorno and Max Horkheimer* in journalism covering the 2016 US presidential election, whose outcome some commentators have ascribed to Donald Trump's* manipulation of social media and reliance on a theatrical rhetoric devoid of actual content. Others have gone so far as to assert that Benjamin and his colleagues "knew Trump was coming"—a sensationalist claim that, however, helps explain the resurgence in public interest in their work.

Why Does "The Work of Art" Matter?

"The Work of Art" remains a seminal text for understanding the source of various arguments around the relationship between technological development, artistic production, politics, and public life that preoccupy scholars across the humanities and social sciences. Benjamin's identification of the effects that film and photography, including their mode of reception, could have on the public, and his recognition that medium matters as much as content, anticipated the ideas of later media theorists. His concern for the ways in which the reproducibility of an artwork might impinge upon our valuation of it, but also potentially democratize it and render audiences themselves participants, anticipated later discussions concerning the democratic potential of the Internet and user-generated content. Likewise, his hope that new media might enable a new form of art criticism capable of challenging the status quo will resonate with anyone who has followed the debate about the radical potential of blogging, Facebook, or Twitter.

"The Work of Art" also provides a useful path into engaging with Benjamin's work as a whole. A prolific writer, Benjamin wrote at length about history, politics, art, literature, religion, and, perhaps most famously, capitalism's effects on culture and society. The unorthodox nature of these texts, which move between disciplines and are written in an often maddeningly enigmatic style, makes them difficult to classify—but this is also the reason why Benjamin appeals to scholars working in such different fields. The fact that his ideas have been more widely influential on literary and cultural critics than on philosophers tells us something about their openness and applicability: in some ways, the society Benjamin writes about is not so removed from our own, globalized, digitized context, and the issues concerning art, technology, and power that he expresses remain relevant in the twenty-first century. Beyond academia, then, "The Work of Art" has relevance to anyone attempting to make sense of the polarization and fragmentation of political discourse today and the effects of new media and art on public life.

NOTES

1   Walter Benjamin, "The Work of Art in the Age of Mechanical Reproduction" in *Illuminations*, ed. Hannah Arendt, (London:Pimlico, 1999).

2   Walter Benjamin, "Theses on the Philosophy of History," in *Illuminations*, ed. Hannah Arendt, (London: Pimlico, 1999).

THE AUTHOR AND THE HISTORICAL CONTEXT

KEY POINTS

- "The Work of Art in the Age of Mechanical Reproduction" is a seminal essay in the history of art criticism, literary studies* and critical theory.*

- Walter Benjamin was a leftist Jewish intellectual whose importance was only recognized several decades after his death.

- Benjamin's essay is a product of the tense years preceding World War II.

Why Read This Text?

In his influential essay, "The Work of Art in the Age of Mechanical Reproduction," the philosopher and cultural critic Walter Benjamin introduces a new set of concepts for understanding the art object in the modern era. Reconfiguring the traditional perspectives of art history* and art criticism, Benjamin argues that the work of art must be understood in relation to the material history of its production (how it came to be made) and in relation to the new ways in which audiences receive it. Benjamin identifies the significance of the emergent forms of photography and film, which allow for works of art to be reproduced and disseminated, and which audiences often experience collectively, and in a fundamentally different way from a painting or a play.

Benjamin argues that reproducibility erodes the "aura"* of artworks: rather than existing in a separate, autonomous sphere (as art historians of the day argued), the work of art in the age of mechanical

> ❝ The pleasure [Benjamin] took in the physical act of writing … was as great as his aversion to mechanical expedients: in this respect the essay 'The Work of Art in the Age of Mechanical Reproduction,' like many other stages of his intellectual biography, was an act of identification with the aggressor. ❞
>
> Theodor Adorno, "Benjamin the Letter Writer"

reproduction is part of everyday life. This is important because the view of art as autonomous,* according to Benjamin, has much in common with fascist rhetoric, which similarly relies on imposing one singular view, upholding social inequality as "natural," and treating life itself as a fixed and unchanging work of art. By contrast, understanding works of art as both a product of political circumstance and capable of shifting it, allows us to recognize art's revolutionary potential. While it went largely ignored for the first three decades following its publication, Benjamin's essay has greatly influenced literary and art criticism and cultural studies* since the 1970s, and has frequently been cited since the beginning of 2016 by journalists responding to the US presidential election and rise of right-wing extremism.1

Author's Life

Walter Benjamin (1892–1940) was a leftist German Jewish philosopher born to an affluent family in Berlin. His father was a banker and an art dealer, who intended that his wealth would support Benjamin throughout adulthood so he would not have to secure paid work. As Hannah Arendt* has noted, this socio-economic privilege was characteristic of an entire generation of German-Jewish intellectuals born at the end of the nineteenth century, whose parents supported them financially so that they could study and write.[2] This wealth contrasted sharply with the poverty Benjamin experienced in later life. The economic depression in Germany following World War I* (also known as the Great Depression*) rendered his father unable to financially support him and his wife, Dora Sophie Pollak.* Benjamin thus struggled in the following decades to find ways to get paid for his writing.[3] These financial struggles also affected his marriage, which lasted only eleven years: he and Dora had a son in 1918, but separated in 1928.

Benjamin spent the years of World War I translating writings of the poet Charles Baudelaire,* which indelibly influenced his interest in the relationship between capitalism,* urbanization,* and art—as manifest in essays such as "Paris, Capital of the Nineteenth Century" (1935; 1939), and "On Some Motifs in Baudelaire." The latter essay was intended to form part of his unfinished magnum opus, *The Arcades Project* (1927–),* a study of the Paris shopping arcades.* Benjamin's translations of Baudelaire were published as *Charles Baudelaire, Tableaux Parisiens* (1923).*

Author's Background

"The Work of Art" is an anti-fascist essay composed during fascism's ascent. In February 1933, the Reichstag,* the building that housed the German Parliament, was set ablaze. The recently elected Chancellor, the anti-Semitic,* anti-communist, and fiercely nationalist politician Adolf Hitler,* used the burning of the Reichstag to pass emergency measures that removed communist opposition (the fire was alleged to have been started by communist insurgents) and ultimately consolidated power for his National Socialist German Workers' Party,* also known as the Nazis, by making them the majority. Paying heed to the increasing violence surrounding this political shift, Benjamin went into exile in March 1933, spending most of the 1930s living in Paris when he had the necessary funds. He also traveled extensively around Europe, often staying with friends and acquaintances in order to fund his writing. He wrote both versions of "The Work of Art" while in

Paris—the first in 1935, and the final version in 1939, just after the Nazis had taken away his German citizenship.[4]

The Nazi invasion of France in 1940, and the Gestapo's subsequent confiscation of Benjamin's vast personal library and a number of his unfinished manuscripts, forced him to flee France. He left his notes for the book he was writing at the time, *The Arcades Project*, with the writer Georges Bataille,* who was librarian at the Bibliothéque nationale de France. Benjamin's plan was to cross the Franco–Spanish border at Portbou, use a Spanish transit visa to travel from Spain to Lisbon, and from there board a ship to the United States, using an emergency visa issued to him as a German refugee in Marseilles by the United States government. A series of misfortunes rendered this plan unfeasible. Thus, on the night of September 26, 1940, upon discovering that the Spanish police were not honoring visas made out in Marseilles, he allegedly committed suicide. Ironically, this act made an impression on the border officials, who allowed his fellow travelers to cross into Spain after all, and within a few weeks the visa embargo was lifted.[5] The very real threat of fascism that Benjamin's generation faced, and that ultimately took his life, forms an important backdrop to "The Work of Art."

NOTES

1   Tom Whyman, "Which Philosophy Can Best Explain 2016?," Vice, December 15, 2016, accessed June 20, 2017, https://www.vice.com/en_uk/article/z4ngy4/which-philosophy-can-help-us-understand-2016; Jeremy Roos, "Trump's victory speaks to a crumbling liberal order," Road, November 9, 2016, accessed June 20, 2017, https://roarmag.org/essays/trump-victory-legitimation-crisis-capitalism/; Stuart Jeffries, "Why a forgotten 1930s critique of capitalism is back in fashion," Guardian, September 9, 2016, accessed June 20, 2017, https://www.theguardian.com/books/2016/sep/09/marxist-critique-capitalism-frankfurt-school-cultural-apocalypse; Alex Ross, "The Frankfurt School knew Trump was Coming," New Yorker, December 5, 2016, accessed June 20, 2017, http://www.newyorker.com/culture/cultural-comment/the-frankfurt-school-knew-trump-was-coming.

2   Hannah Arendt, "Introduction: Walter Benjamin, 1892–1940" (1968), in
    Illuminations, trans. Harry Zohn and ed. Hannah Arendt (London: Pimlico,
    1999 [1970]), 7–60 (31).

3   Howard Eiland and Michael W. Jennings, *Walter Benjamin: A Critical Life*
    (Cambridge, MA: Belknap Press/Harvard University Press, 2013), 3; 221;
    412.

4   Rolf Goebel, "Introduction: Benjamin's Actuality," in *A Companion to the
    Works of Walter Benjamin*, ed. Rolf Goebel (London: Camden House, 2009),
    1–22 (6).

5   Arendt, "Introduction: Walter Benjamin: 1892–1940," 23.

MODULE 2
ACADEMIC CONTEXT

KEY POINTS

- Walter Benjamin's "The Work of Art in the Age of Mechanical Reproduction" draws on Western Marxism,* Surrealism,* and Dada* while refuting Futurism.*

- While a number of Benjamin's colleagues sought to challenge fascism and capitalist ideology, not all of these scholars shared Benjamin's optimism about mass culture.*

- The philosophers Theodor Adorno and Max Horkheimer and the playwright Bertolt Brecht* were among Benjamin's greatest influences.

The Work in Its Context

"The Work of Art" is very difficult to categorize, as it incorporates ideas from a range of disciplines to challenge the very terms by which art, politics, and culture should be discussed. However, Western Marxism,* Dada, Surrealism, and Futurism loom largest in the text.

Building on the work of political theorist Karl Marx, Marxist critics approach cultural phenomena in relation to the material conditions that produce them. They are concerned by the ways in which capitalism mediates our relationship with the people, places and things around us. Expanding upon Marx's idea of commodity fetishism*[1]—that human relations under capitalism become transactional—Georg Lukács argued that under capitalism, objects are valued over and above the people who made them.[2] Benjamin's essay extends Lukács's ideas, but differs in its identification of the radical possibilities that the loss of the artwork's aura opens up.

> **❝** The history of every art form shows critical epochs in which a certain art form aspires to effects which could be fully obtained only with a changed technical standard ... Dadaism attempted to create by pictorial— and literary—means the effects which the public today seeks in the film. **❞**
>
> Walter Benjamin, "The Work of Art in the Age of Mechanical Reproduction"

Surrealism and Dada were two related movements in literature and the visual arts that Benjamin wrote about at length throughout the 1920s,[3] and which were greatly influenced by Marxist thought. These artists sought to create works that would scandalize viewers, shocking them out of their daily routines and forcing them to reassess what they knew. They did this to challenge capitalist culture, which, like their Marxist critic contemporaries, they saw as creating a population of sleepwalking consumer-citizens disincentivized from questioning their political leaders or the lifestyle imposed on them. Benjamin explicitly mentions Dada's shock tactics in his essay, seeing them as the precursor to the special effects afforded by film.

Futurism was an artistic movement that developed in Italy around the same time as Surrealism and Dada. However, where the former two aligned themselves with socialist* views, the latter championed nationalism,* fascism, and violence. In particular, Futurists saw speed, technology, and capitalist progress as means to make Italy a leader on the global stage. They famously called war "the world's only hygiene"[4]—change could only be brought about through the destruction of past traditions by violent means. When Benjamin challenges the "aestheticization of politics"—the use of pageantry and spectacle to make the masses feel allegiance to the nation state and ignore their own suffering—he is also challenging Futurism's celebration of these methods.

Overview of the Field

While his approach was innovative, Benjamin was not alone in challenging the rise of fascism or capitalism's effects on culture. Rather, he formed part of a group of anti-fascist Marxist scholars working at the Institute for Social Research led by Max Horkheimer and Theodor Adorno. Scholars associated with the Institute for Social Research are referred to today as the "Frankfurt School,"* after the University of Frankfurt, where it was originally based. The Institute moved to New York City in 1934 to escape Nazi persecution. As well as publishing "The Work of Art," the Institute funded some of Benjamin's other work.

Perhaps the best-known work to emerge from the Frankfurt School is Adorno and Horkheimer's *Dialectic of Enlightenment: Philosophical Fragments* (1947). One of the essays in this collection, "The Culture Industry: Enlightenment as Mass Deception,"* examines similar themes to Benjamin's "The Work of Art," but argues that popular culture renders people passive consumers rather than critically and politically engaged citizens. Popular film and fiction simply recycles the same themes and storylines over and over again, since tried-and-tested formulae are guaranteed to make money. The end result is a society in which art is treated like a consumer product. This argument was very different from Benjamin's. Where Benjamin sees the new media of his day as a potential means to oppose fascism, Adorno sees no hope: photography and film, he argues, have already been co-opted* to lull citizens into submission. Film doesn't shock viewers into recognizing they are oppressed: rather, it offers an escape from reality that in turn serves the needs of capitalism, since viewers return home from the movies satisfied and once again willing to accept the status quo. While the essay collection was published after Benjamin's death, Adorno expressed some of these ideas in his letters to Benjamin, where he also criticized "The Work of Art" as overly optimistic.[5]

Academic Influences

The ideas of the Marxist German playwright Bertolt Brecht, whom Benjamin met in the late 1920s, were also highly influential on Benjamin's work. In Hannah Arendt's words, Benjamin saw Brecht as "the poet who was most at home in this [the twentieth] century."[6] For Benjamin, Brecht exemplified what was needed of artists at the time: "A total absence of illusion about the age and at the same time an unlimited commitment to it."[7] By this he meant that Brecht was at once aware of the severity of the rise of fascism and the threats of unchecked capitalism, and committed to fighting these—virtues that Benjamin celebrates in "The Work of Art."

Benjamin wrote about Brecht in a series of essays that were only published posthumously in 1966. Here he identified the significance of the "standstill:"* a moment in Brecht's theatrical productions when the actions are interrupted, thus forcing the audience to "take up a position"[8] by "expos[ing] the present" and "alienating* [them] in a lasting manner, through thought, from the conditions in which [they] liv[e]."[9] In "The Work of Art," Benjamin likewise expresses the need for art that will make us critically reflect, but without falling into the trap of self-absorbed contemplation.

Finally, Benjamin was influenced by the work of the late-nineteenth-century Austrian art historian Alois Riegl,* and particularly by the methods that Riegl used in his book, *Late Roman Art Industry* (1905).* For Benjamin, Riegl's work stood out in its recognition that the characteristics of the marketplace in which an artist was operating needed to be addressed alongside more conventional aesthetic concerns, such as genre* or technique.*[10] Because he was more interested in the conditions of artistic production, Riegl paid attention to works of art that usually had been neglected by art historians, but which he identified as important cultural artifacts. This alternative emphasis forms a pivotal component of Benjamin's essay.

NOTES

1   Karl Marx, "The fetishism of commodities and the secret thereof," *Capital: An abridged edition*, ed. David McLellan (Oxford: Oxford University Press, 2008 [1867]), 42–50.

2   Georg Lukács, *History and Class Consciousness: Studies in Marxist Dialectics* (London: Merlin, 1968 [1923]), 83.

3   Walter Benjamin, "Surrealism" (1929), reprinted in *One-Way Street and Other Writings*, ed. Amit Chaudhuri and trans. J. A. Underwood (London: Penguin, 2009), 143–60; Walter Benjamin, "Dream Kitsch: Gloss on Surrealism" (1925), reprinted in *The Work of Art in the Age of its Technical Reproducibility and Other Writings*, ed. Michael W. Jennings et al, trans. Edmund Jephcott, Rodney Livingstone, Howard Eiland et al. (Cambridge, MA: Belknap/Harvard University Press, 2008), 236–39.

4   Tommaso Marinetti, "Futurist Manifesto" (1908), in *Theories of Modern Art: A Source Book by Artists and Critics*, ed. Herschel B. Chipp (Berkeley, CA: University of California Press, 1996 [1968]), 286.

5   Theodor W. Adorno and Walter Benjamin, *The Complete Correspondence: 1928–40*, trans. Nicholas Walker (Cambridge: Polity, 1999), 127–34.

6   Erdmut Wizislda, *Walter Benjamin and Bertolt Brecht: The Story of a Friendship*, trans. Christine Shuttleworth (New Haven: Yale University Press), 103.

7   Wizislda, *Walter Benjamin and Bertolt Brecht*, 103.

8   Walter Benjamin, *Understanding Brecht*, trans. Anna Bostock (London: Verso, 1998), 100.

9   Benjamin, *Understanding Brecht*, 100.

10 T. Y. Levin, "Walter Benjamin and the Theory of Art History," *October* 47 (Winter 1988): 77–83; Mike Gubster, *Time's Visible Surface: Alois Riegl and the Discourse on History and Temporality in Fin-de-Siécle Vienna* (Detroit, MI: Wayne State University Press, 2006), 20; 202; 208–12.

MODULE 3
THE PROBLEM

KEY POINTS

- Walter Benjamin's "The Work of Art in the Age of Mechanical Reproduction" investigates the political ramifications of the processes of technological reproduction.*
- "The Work of Art" challenges received ideas about art's autonomy, while building on the work of Marxist critics.
- Benjamin argues that the idealized view of art as unchanging and everlasting can be easily manipulated to uphold the status quo.

Core Question

In what ways do the processes of technological reproduction available in the first decades of the twentieth century alter the production and reception of works of art? What are the political consequences of these altered states?

While fascism was very much at the forefront of public and scholarly debate during this politically charged period, the questions Benjamin addresses in "The Work of Art" were not. His essay was therefore highly original. Benjamin attempts to address these questions by analyzing the changing status of what he terms the "aura" that surrounds works of art through an exploration of the relationship of that aura to technology and the historical context. "That which withers in the age of mechanical reproduction is the aura of the work of art," he argues.[1]

While Benjamin does not explicitly define the "aura," the essay makes clear that it is connected to art's historical association with the

> ❝ Earlier much futile thought had been devoted to the question of whether photography is an art. The primary question—whether the very invention of photography had not transformed the entire nature of art—was not raised. ❞
>
> Walter Benjamin, "The Work of Art in the Age of Mechanical Reproduction"

rituals of the church or monarchy (what Benjamin calls its "cult" value), and to the ideas of authenticity and autonomy that have been traditionally attributed to great art works. When a work of art can be reproduced in a book or as a postcard, the uniqueness of its location as an object occupying one specific place that people travel from far and wide to visit is undermined. Reproduction allows the work of art in the modern age to be re-appropriated—pinned to a bedroom wall, sent to a distant relative, juxtaposed with advertisements for coffee. This capacity for reproduction has a democratizing effect. More than this, new technologies have delivered new art forms, such as film and photography, that no longer require a unique or original object. There is no "original" film reel or photograph: all copies are equal.

The Participants

Benjamin's essay engages with two sets of received ideas. First, it challenges the idea of the work of art that was still dominant in traditional art criticism, where the work of art was studied as an autonomous object located in a separate sphere from the material realities of the everyday world. While capable of reflecting the context in which it was created, such an object was considered to qualify as a work of art thanks to its uniqueness, which allowed it to *transcend* that context. It was as if it contained some transmissible kernel of eternal and unchanging value that also reflected its authenticity and uniqueness. The aura that this idea gave to the work of art isolated it from the subsequent contexts in which it was viewed and received.

The second set of received ideas is Western Marxism—a term coined by the philosopher Maurice Merleau-Ponty* to refer to elaborations of Marx's ideas in Western and Central Europe. Benjamin's essay offers a radical critique of capitalism as well as art history, for he identifies how concepts relating to how art has been traditionally viewed help to support capitalism and fascism. This approach, which concentrates on cultural production rather than the formal techniques of art, has much in common with other thinkers with whom Benjamin was in dialogue.

The Contemporary Debate

Benjamin's essay argues that the idealized versions of art upheld by traditional art history can easily be deployed to sustain and naturalize massive social inequalities. The persistence of separating art from its various contexts forms part of a wider process that enables the dominant culture to limit the possibility of changing the status quo. It also enables that dominant culture to incorporate and neutralize dissent.

Against the backdrop of an ascending fascism, Benjamin's essay reveals the potentially dire political consequences of defending a traditional notion of an art work as something authentic, autonomous, eternal, and unchanging: for these are the same terms the Nazis also used to justify their violence and oppression. For Benjamin, such a position aestheticizes politics: it allows leaders to dupe the public into thinking of the nation state itself as an unchanging and unchangeable work of art. He wants to reverse this to show how it is possible to instead politicize art and instigate radical political action on a mass scale.

Benjamin thus seeks to link the study of art to the wider social and cultural processes that impact upon its production (how it is made), reception (how it is viewed), and reproduction (how it is disseminated). Examining the work of art in relation to this wider context enables

27

him to consider the critical limitations and political consequences of a more traditional approach. It also enables him to establish an innovative set of approaches to art history that reflect his engagement with the Marxist study of culture. Benjamin, however, diverges from fellow Marxist thinkers, such as Siegfried Kracauer* and Theodor Adorno, who viewed mass culture as a source of distraction that ultimately prevents citizens from engaging politically: instead, he sees it as holding the potential for radical change. Where Kracauer and Adorno view new media as further tools of capitalist exploitation, Benjamin argues that new media has the capacity to shock people into action.

NOTES

1   Walter Benjamin, "The Work of Art in the Age of Mechanical Reproduction," in *Illuminations*, ed. Hannah Arendt (London: Pimlico, 1999), 215.

THE AUTHOR'S CONTRIBUTION

KEY POINTS

- "The Work of Art in the Age of Mechanical Reproduction" formulates a theory of art criticism that cannot be co-opted by fascism, and might be used to instigate social change.

- The advent of new media and changes in art's reception are transforming the public's perception of art and communication.

- Benjamin's unique argument involves appropriating quotes from previous sources in a process resembling collage* or montage.*

Author's Aims

Walter Benjamin's "The Work of Art in the Age of Mechanical Reproduction" was purposefully designed to combat fascism, or, at least, to formulate a way of critiquing, and thinking about, modern art that could not be co-opted by fascists. The need for such a work had become increasingly apparent as the ruling Nazi party in Germany deployed fascist policies that suppressed civil liberties and persecuted specific sections of the population, primarily the large and diverse Jewish community that included Benjamin's family. Benjamin's analysis of the work of art in an age of new technologies of production, reception, and reproduction, is thus an attempt to identify ways in which the art generated by new technologies might serve the interests of those alienated and oppressed by the dominant regimes of capitalism and right-wing extremism in the Western world, be this by enabling outright revolution or by opening up more democratic ways of thinking about art and culture as a whole.

> ❝ During long periods of history, the mode of human sense perception changes with humanity's entire mode of existence. The manner in which human sense perception is organized, the medium in which it is accomplished, is determined not only by nature but by historical circumstances as well. ❞
>
> Walter Benjamin, "The Work of Art in the Age of Mechanical Reproduction"

Benjamin's optimism regarding the radical potential of mass culture (namely film, but also photography, magazines, and popular fiction) was dramatically different from that of his fellow Marxist scholars, and indeed from that of more conservative art critics of the period. Those associated with the Frankfurt School thought that mass culture promoted passivity—a population of distracted, uncritical consumer-viewers switched off from politics—and could be used to control public opinion. Conservative art critics instead saw it as killing the intellect and imagination: they urged their middle-class readers to stay away from the "trash" consumed by the lower classes. Art critics further perceived these new forms as taking away their own authority as experts: as Benjamin himself notes, "it is inherent in the technique of the film as well as that of sports that everybody who witnesses its accomplishments is somewhat of an expert."[1] They viewed this leveling of the playing field as a threat. Benjamin's essay was thus original both in its analysis of reproducibility and in his optimistic view of its ramifications.

Approach

Benjamin's unusual approach involves setting out a series of ideas in fourteen distinct "theses,"* or condensed mini-essays, in which he analyses not only the history of artistic reproduction and the erosion of the art object's "aura," but also specific technical features of photography and film, the changing relationship between audience and medium, and the radical potential of distraction. The essay thus unspools as a series of different arguments that together show connections between the specific characteristics of the new media he is discussing, and a broader shift in the public's relationship to art and rhetoric* (the ways in which messages are expressed).The originality of this argument lies in the fact that for Benjamin, the very features of photograph and film that render them inauthentic forms will, in turn, change the public's reception of *all* forms of performance and expression—not only painting, music, or theater, but also the speeches, parades, and other public displays mounted by fascist leaders to instill allegiance to the state. Benjamin argues that exposure to new media will result in a new skepticism towards aesthetics (art and display) as a whole, leading people to recognize when spectacle is being used by their leaders to manipulate public opinion. Thus, for Benjamin, the erosion of traditional artworks' authority following the advent of new media, and the shifts in public reception of artworks, have the potential to bring about new forms of opposition to fascism. Such a view was unprecedented.

Contribution in Context

While a highly original essay, "The Work of Art" bears the imprint of numerous thinkers. This is attested in the essay's famous first line, "When Marx undertook his critique of the capitalistic mode of production,* this mode was in its infancy,"[2] as well as in the many citations of writers, philosophers, and critics. As in Benjamin's other work, the reference to Marx and proliferation of quotes from other texts aims to situate his argument within Marxist discourse as well as to respond to debates in art and literary criticism occurring at the time. Thus, for example, the essay's epigraph (the quote that comes before the

opening sentence) is from French poet and essayist Paul Valéry's*
(1871–1945) essay, "The Conquest of Ubiquity" (1928),* in which
Valéry speculates about the likely effects of new technologies on culture
at large.[3]

Benjamin later quotes another passage from this same essay: "Just as
water, gas, and electricity are brought into our houses from far off to
satisfy our needs in response to a minimal effort, so we shall be supplied
with visual or auditory images, which will appear and disappear at a
simple movement of the hand, hardly more than a sign."[4] However,
where Valéry's text is referring to the rapidity with which technology is
likely to transform people's lives beyond the point of recognition,
Benjamin uses the passage to support his view that traditional art forms
anticipate the new technologies that follow.

This method of attributing new meaning to other writers' words is
characteristic of Benjamin, who does not quote other writers in order
to adopt their arguments, but instead interprets their words in new ways
that ultimately serve his own, often very different, viewpoint. This
approach resembles the techniques of visual collage and cinematic and
literary montage in which Benjamin was so interested. Both forms
involve juxtaposing fragments of (usually unrelated) material from
different sources to create new meanings. Readers today may in turn
find themselves interpreting these de-contextualised quotes somewhat
differently—for example, the quote from Valéry's essay seems to eerily
predict the advent of the Internet.

NOTES

1   Walter Benjamin, "The Work of Art in the Age of Mechanical Reproduction," in
    Illuminations, ed. Hannah Arendt (London: Pimlico, 1999), 225.

2   Benjamin, "The Work of Art," 211.

3   Paul Valéry, "The Conquest of Ubiquity" (1928) in *Aesthetics*, trans. Ralph
    Manheim (New York: Pantheon Books, 1964), 226, quoted in "The Work of
    Art," 211.

MODULE 5
MAIN IDEAS

KEY POINTS

- "The Work of Art in the Age of Mechanical Reproduction" is concerned with the effects that new technologies enabling artworks to be reproduced are having on society.

- Benjamin shows how reproducibility renders art more accessible, challenges traditional art criticism, and can instigate political change.

- Benjamin's fragmentary writing style is in keeping with the nonconformist approach to criticism he is promoting.

Key Themes

The main themes in Benjamin's essay involve the relationships between the work of art, technologies of reproduction, and political change. Technological changes that enable multiple copies of an art work to be reproduced challenge traditional notions of the work of art as an autonomous object imbued with an "aura" of authenticity and unchanging value. Benjamin argues that with the mass dissemination of images, the "aura" attached to the work of art is eroded. Disconnected from church and monarchy, and rendered more widely available, the work of art is democratized.

Benjamin connects this argument to a longer historical shift, from the work of art's status as a ritual object—either through magic, religion, or as an object of beauty to be passively contemplated—to its new status: as a political object. Benjamin outlines a related shift within this historical perspective as the artwork changes from having cult value (as a ritual object) to exhibition value (as an object to be

> 66 [T]he instant the criterion of authenticity ceases to be applicable to artistic production, the total function of art is reversed. Instead of being based on ritual, it begins to be based on another practice—politics. 99
>
> Walter Benjamin, "The Work of Art in the Age of Mechanical Reproduction"

showcased). In the modern era, he argues, art will be used to either manipulate the masses into submission or enable their liberation.

For Benjamin, film and photography have affected the ways in which we perceive and experience the world, and have the capacity to challenge oppressive regimes. This is because film's obvious lack of authenticity—the fact that there is nothing to distinguish a film's "original" reel from its copies, and that the medium itself is in fact designed for reproduction and dissemination—renders audiences more aware of other artificial displays, such as the parades that totalitarian leaders use to dupe the public into submission (what Benjamin calls the "aestheticization of politics"). According to Benjamin, the differences in how audiences watch film compared to traditional art forms will affect how they experience other forms of display, including propaganda: "The public is an examiner, but an absent-minded one."[1]

Exploring the Ideas

Benjamin explores the idea of the "aura" in Theses One and Two of his essay. While all art is reproducible, an imitation of a painting does not erode the original's authority since it can easily be revealed to be a fake. Technological reproductions, by contrast, can exist independently to the original: first, by using close ups to bring out details not immediately evident in the original, and second, by enabling the original to be shared elsewhere.[2]

As well as resulting in the aura's depreciation, these characteristics will inevitably change people's perception of the world around them. In fact, Benjamin argues, film will change "humanity's entire mode of existence"[3] and for this reason it is the pre-eminent "mode of human sense perception" of the twentieth century.[4] Its most influential aspects are its mass reception (people watch films collectively, and the movie industry reaches far more members of the public than gallery exhibitions can), and the possibilities it allows for audiences to see the world around them in far sharper focus.

Theses Four and Five introduce the outmodedness of "Art for Art's Sake:"* the idea that art should be revered uncritically, and considered to be elevated above its spectators, which Benjamin argues preserves art's ritual function. Reproducibility injects political meaning into artwork, Benjamin contends. Eugène Atget's* photographs in the 1900s, for example, were used in magazine and newspaper articles as "standard evidence for historical occurrences," in turn "acquir[ing] a political significance."[5]

Benjamin also notes that film, like the newspaper, allows for audience participation, which causes "the distinction between author and public … to lose its basic character."[6] More specifically: "Any man today can lay claim to being filmed;"[7] likewise, "today there is hardly a gainfully employed European who could not, in principle, find an opportunity to publish somewhere or other."[8] Benjamin's concern here is not, however, with the potential for photography or film to communicate radical ideas (which he notes can be co-opted by the companies that publish or produce them), so much as for the potential for "a revolutionary criticism of traditional concepts of art."[9] While these new forms themselves may not be able to instigate social change, they can help dismantle old ways of understanding art that risk upholding oppressive social structures.

Finally, and most contentiously, Benjamin proposes that new media's alleged diminishing of the viewing public's attention span and capacity to absorb information should be seen as a good thing. Distraction* is a way to ignore the many stimuli of mass culture (advertising billboards, shop window displays, tabloid newspaper headlines) and preserve one's energy to attend to important content and political action. The distraction triggered by moving pictures is a way to counteract capitalist culture's imposition on the individual's mental energies, and should be seen as a tool for good.

Language and Expression

Benjamin's friend and collaborator Theodor Adorno, wrote that Benjamin was the "unsurpassed master" at a form of essay writing in which each theme builds upon its predecessor to construct a coherent argument.[10] Adorno clarifies his statement by explaining that in such essays, thought "does not progress in a single direction; instead, the moments are interwoven as in a carpet. The fruitfulness of the thoughts depends on the density of the texture."[11] Elsewhere, Adorno commented that Benjamin's "philosophy of fragmentation remained itself fragmentary," a victim of its preferred method. For Adorno, that method "cannot be separated from its content."[12]

This fragmented approach is apparent in "The Work of Art," which is divided into fourteen separate theses, a prologue and an epilogue—an approach that prevents the reader from differentiating between the form of his work (its literary features) and its content (what it says). This is important because Benjamin himself views the distinction between form and content to be both old-fashioned and politically suspect: the two must be examined in conjunction with each other. Benjamin's unorthodox argument thus finds an equivalent in the unorthodox style of the text itself, which does not propose a single, coherent, and overarching point, but rather various loosely connected ideas. This style in turn prevents the reader from drawing final conclusions, which is one reason why Benjamin's work continues to be discussed.

NOTES

1   Walter Benjamin, "The Work of Art in the Age of Mechanical Reproduction," in *Illuminations*, ed. Hannah Arendt (London: Pimlico, 1999), 234.

2   Benjamin, "The Work of Art," 214.

3   Benjamin, "The Work of Art," 216.

4   Benjamin, "The Work of Art," 216.

5   Benjamin, "The Work of Art," 220.

6   Benjamin, "The Work of Art," 225.

7   Benjamin, "The Work of Art," 225.

8   Benjamin, "The Work of Art," 225.

9   Benjamin, "The Work of Art," 224.

10 Theodor W. Adorno, "The Essay as Form," in *Notes to Literature: Volume One*, trans. Shierry Weber Nicholsen (New York: Columbia University, 1991), 3–23 (13).

11 Adorno, "The Essay as Form," 13.

12 Theodor W. Adorno, "A Portrait of Walter Benjamin," in *Prisms*, trans. Samuel and Shierry Weber (Cambridge, MA; MIT, 1988), 227–42 (239).

MODULE 6
SECONDARY IDEAS

KEY POINTS

- "The Work of Art in the Age of Mechanical Reproduction" also examines the effects of photography, film, and technological innovation more broadly on our perception of the world around us.

- Benjamin shows how the camera alters the relationship between actor and audience, reveals aspects of the world hitherto hidden, and is at once absorbing and immersive, and yet experienced distractedly.

- While Benjamin intended his essay to be a political critique, it has largely been read as a work of art criticism: thus, his central points have also been the most overlooked.

Other Ideas

While the "The Work of Art in the Age of Mechanical Reproduction" is, at heart, about how art criticism might be used to resist fascism, it is also a study of the transformative effects of specific techniques in film and photography on our perception of the world around us—and a meditation on technology itself. While these points are secondary to Benjamin's concepts of the aura, politicized art, and aestheticized politics, they are nevertheless important for an exhaustive understanding of both the essay and his broader body of work. Of particular note are his examination of the camera's mediation of the traditional relationship between actor and audience; his assessment of its revelation of aspects of the world that would otherwise remain hidden; and his contention that the collective viewing aspect makes spectators more amenable to experimental films than they would be to experimental paintings, which are viewed singly and by a middle-class demographic that still responds to the authority of art critics.

> ❝ Unmistakably, reproduction as offered by picture magazines and newsreels differs from the image seen by the unarmed eye. Uniqueness and permanence are as closely linked in the latter as are transitoriness and reproducibility in the former. ❞
>
> Walter Benjamin, "The Work of Art in the Age of Mechanical Reproduction"

In Thesis Seven, Benjamin notes that when photography first emerged, critics were concerned with "whether photography was an art. The primary question—whether the very invention of photography had not transformed the entire nature of art—was not raised."[1] His essay thus broaches this transformation.

Exploring the Ideas

Film, Benjamin argues, has transformed the traditional relationship between actor and audience by the use of the camera. The camera manipulates the appearance of the actors and their actions by changing angles and through the use of close-ups, while the actions themselves are often filmed in stages and only assembled later: all of this creates distance between audience and actors. "The audience's identification with the actor is really an identification with the camera."[2] Likewise, since film actors do not perform for people sitting in front of them, whose responses might alter their performance from one show to the next, the relationship between the cast and viewers is more like that between a shelf of consumer goods and their eventual buyers. During shooting, "the actor has as little contact with [the audience] as any article made in a factory."[3]

At the same time, however, film allows for the examination of minutiae—details in the landscape, in a person's gait, or the sound of a faucet dripping—that we would not be able to perceive otherwise. He compares this ability to isolate details to the skills of the psychoanalyst.

Psychoanalysis* contends that an individual's life is composed of both their conscious thoughts and actions, and the hundreds and thousands of impulses, desires, and aversions of which they are completely unaware because they occur subconsciously. Like the psychoanalyst with the individual's mind, film reveals aspects of the world of which we were not conscious before. The ability to slow down or speed up a filmed sequence affords us a completely new understanding of the subject captured. "The camera introduces us to unconscious optics as does psychoanalysis to unconscious impulses."[4]

Likewise, film affords an immersive experience: comparing the painter to a magician, the cameraman to a surgeon, and reality to a sick body undergoing treatment, Benjamin notes in Thesis Eleven that the painter, like the magician moving his hands over a sick body without touching it, remains at a "natural distance from reality," while the cameraman, like the surgeon cutting into the body, "penetrates deeply" into it.[5]

Elsewhere, Benjamin makes a comparison between film's immersive quality, which the audience experiences distractedly, with that of architecture. This connects to a broader point about the time lag between the most advanced artistic practices and technology. Art, he argues, anticipates shifts that subsequent technologies will make more widespread and more mainstream: "just as lithography virtually implied the illustrated newspaper, so did photography foreshadow the sound film."[6] By the same token, a city dweller's distracted experience of architecture, which they move through without properly observing, is akin to that of the movie-going public, who is "an examiner, but an absent-minded one."[7]

Such points indirectly feed back into the main themes of Benjamin's essay in relation to the effect of technological reproducibility on the production and reception of the work of art, and on modern experience and perception more generally.

Overlooked

The political dimension of Benjamin's argument was marginalized for many years. The history of the different versions of the essay emphasizes this point. Benjamin's references to Marx and his explicit subscription to socialism and opposition to fascism were initially suppressed. However, even the most popular English-language version of the essay—a version that includes these references—has, in the words of Benjamin scholar Susan Buck-Morss,* been "read, in the United States at least, as a thoroughly depoliticized* defense of the culture industry" rather than an attempt to use mass culture to oppose totalitarianism.*[8] Benjamin's essay, Morss argues, is a manifesto of political aesthetics:* it demonstrates how any discussion of art is already political. To ignore the political dimension of Benjamin's argument is to miss the whole point of the essay.

Approaching Benjamin's essay as a political manifesto in turn makes it easier to see the connections between it and other important essays he wrote, such as "The Author as Producer"* and "Theses on the Philosophy of History,"* which seek to reveal the political dimension of cultural production (in this case, artistic production and the writing of history).

Beyond this glaring omission, however, Benjamin's essay has been thoroughly mined by scholars both within Benjamin studies and in other disciplines, who have eagerly applied its ideas in the discussion of new and emergent technologies. One might even argue—as Morss does in the above-mentioned speech—that Benjamin's essay has been *overly* used, often at the cost of diluting its original ideas.

NOTES

1   Walter Benjamin, "The Work of Art in the Age of Mechanical Reproduction," in *Illuminations*, ed. Hannah Arendt (London: Pimlico, 1999), 220.

2   Benjamin, "The Work of Art," 222.

3   Benjamin, "The Work of Art," 224.

4   Benjamin, "The Work of Art," 230.

5   Benjamin, "The Work of Art," 227.

6   Benjamin, "The Work of Art," 213.

7   Benjamin, "The Work of Art," 234.

8   Susan Buck-Morss, "Anti-Stalinist Art: Benjamin, Shostakovich, and the
     End of the Story," Keynote lecture of the first Congress of the International
     Walter Benjamin Association, Amsterdam, July 1997. Published as
     "Revolutionary Time: The Vanguard and the Avant-Garde" in *Benjamin
     Studies*, Studien 1, ed. Helga Geyer Ryan (Amsterdam: Rodopi, 2002).
     http://susanbuckmorss.info/text/antistalinist-art/. Accessed July 13, 2017.

MODULE 7
ACHIEVEMENT

KEY POINTS

- "The Work of Art in the Age of Mechanical Reproduction" is a highly influential essay despite its overly optimistic assessment of mass culture and new media.
- Benjamin's essay engaged in original ways with contemporary debates around the status of film and photography and the rise of fascism.
- "The Work of Art" failed to anticipate how the art market would eventually commercialize the aura of authenticity of artworks.

Assessing the Argument

As the title of Benjamin's essay intimates, "The Work of Art in the Age of Mechanical Reproduction" puts as much emphasis on technology as the work of art. Benjamin's essay traces the origins of transformations and changes in perception in the modern era to new techniques and creative practices. At this level, the essay has proved to have an unexpected relevance for a digital age in which new technologies—computers, the Internet, mobile phones—have fundamentally altered the way we interact with the world (as well as on the technologically inflected ways that artists produce their work).[1]

However, Benjamin's emphasis on film as the key revolutionary medium driving this cultural shift has proved romantically optimistic given the spectacularly reactionary* and formulaic quality of mainstream cinema. The manufactured aura around the film star that he identifies in his essay perpetuates the same kind of separation between the audience and performer that Benjamin hoped would be

> **❝** [F]or the first time in world history, mechanical reproduction emancipates the work of art from its parasitical dependence on ritual. To an ever greater degree the work of art reproduced becomes the work of art designed for reproducibility. From a photographic negative, for example, one can make any number of prints; to ask for the 'authentic' print makes no sense. **❞**
>
> Walter Benjamin, "The Work of Art in the Age of Mechanical Reproduction"

countered by the potentially liberating techniques of montage (whereby the story is told through the juxtaposition of short, segmented clips) and other optical effects. These effects have, instead, failed to jolt the viewer from a passive contemplation of a seemingly unchanging and unchangeable system into engaging in a more active transformation of the world.[2]

Achievement in Context

The publication and reception of Benjamin's essay were greatly affected by the political tensions of the period—to the extent that the first version to be published was altered to prevent alienating its intended readership. Most notably, the references to the work of Karl Marx in the opening lines of the early versions of the essay were eliminated by the editors at the Institute for Social Research as they prepared a translation of the unpublished essay to appear in French.[3] References to "fascism" were altered to the less explicit "totalitarian regimes."[4] After much discussion, and due to his desperate financial situation, Benjamin reluctantly accepted the editorial changes. This was partly because he wanted to find an outlet for his thoughts at a time when many former channels of publication had been closed to him by the dictates of the Nazis: publishing with the Institute for Social Research, in other words, was his last chance. The English version that is the primary focus of this analysis is a translation of the third version of the essay in which the reference to Marx and fascism are restored (and which includes a longer discussion of the significance of film for a cultural and political analysis of art and technology).

The editorial softening of Benjamin's revolutionary tone in the essay reflects the Institute's efforts to not alienate their new host country (the Institute moved to New York City in 1934 to avoid Nazi persecution).[5] The changes are also evidence of critical points of disagreement between Benjamin and the Institute's leaders. In particular, Adorno saw Benjamin's contact with Bertolt Brecht as contaminating the originality of the essay's insights with a certain kind of romantic optimism.[6] According to Adorno, Brecht's influence led Benjamin to adopt an overly optimistic idea of a spontaneous revolutionary potential contained in the new technologies of reproduction rather than engaging in a more theoretically systematic analysis.[7] The version the Institute published was thus a compromise between Adorno's more critical view of mass culture and Benjamin's radical optimistic one.

Limitations

It could be argued that Benjamin's focus on specific forms of technologically reproducible works of art—photography and film—and on the historical shifts that instigated or resulted from their development, limits its applicability. In an age where such media as photography and film have become increasingly integrated with other technologies, some of Benjamin's thesis is arguably less important than it was when he first conceived it.

It is likewise necessary to point out that the changes Benjamin envisaged new technologies could bring about have not come to pass. The very "shock" effects that Benjamin identifies in montage, close-ups, and special effects, have become a hallmark of mainstream cinema that the audience expects. Benjamin saw special effects as the equivalent to the shock value that Dada and Surrealism sought to provoke through their experimental art works, which were intended to prevent the kind of contemplation and studied critique that more traditional paintings afford.[8] Dadaists sought to "outrage the public" by making their art works "the center of scandal"[9]—the most famous example of this is Marcel Duchamp's* decision to sign and exhibit a urinal. Rather than pleasing the eye, "the work of art of the Dadaists became an instrument of ballistics. It hit the spectator like a bullet, it happened to him."[10] By contrast, just as Surrealism and Dada are now seen as integral parts of art history and exhibited in some of the most famous art museums, the optics Benjamin views to be revolutionary have become commonplace. Similarly, Benjamin's analysis of the aura that withers around the work of art in an age of technological reproducibility seems unable to account for the blockbuster art exhibitions that tour the globe and attract millions of visitors. Such exhibitions successfully market the authenticity of the original work of art as a literally unique selling point.

NOTES

1   Anca Pusca, ed. Walter Benjamin and the *Aesthetics of Change* (New York and Basingstoke: Palgrave Macmillan, 2010), esp. Konstantinos Vassiliou, "The Aura of Art After the Advent of the Digital," 158–70.

2   Susan Sontag, "The Decay of Cinema," *New York Times* (February 25, 1996). http://www.nytimes.com/books/00/03/12/specials/sontag-cinema.html. Accessed July 13, 2017.

3   Esther Leslie, "The Work of Art in the Age of Unbearable Capitulation," in *Walter Benjamin: Overpowering Conformism* (London: Reaktion, 2000), 130–67.

4   Leslie, "The Work of Art in the Age of Unbearable Capitulation," 131.

5   Leslie, "The Work of Art in the Age of Unbearable Capitulation," 130 and 131.

6   Theodor W. Adorno and Walter Benjamin, *The Complete Correspondence: 1928–40*, trans. Nicholas Walker (Cambridge: Polity, 1999), 127–34 (130).

MODULE 8
PLACE IN THE AUTHOR'S WORK

KEY POINTS

- The final version of "The Work of Art in the Age of Mechanical Reproduction" was Benjamin's penultimate work, published a year before his alleged suicide.

- "The Work of Art" builds on previous ideas that Benjamin explored in his essays on photography and literature and the Paris arcades.

- Benjamin's best-known essay has become less central as previously unpublished writing by the author has come to light.

Positioning

Completed in 1939, only a year before his suspected suicide, the third and final version of "The Work of Art" is one of Benjamin's last works. However, the essay's focus on the conditions of the production of art, photography, and film, and on the political ramifications of art, relates to themes present throughout Benjamin's work. In particular, the essay builds on his earlier essay, "A Small History of Photography,"[1] where he explored a shift in the physical act of seeing brought about by photography. In this earlier essay he argued that "the destruction of the aura is the mark of a perception whose sense of the sameness of things has grown to the point where even the singular, the unique, is divested of its uniqueness—by means of its reproduction."[2] He also proposed the concept of the "optical unconscious"[3] that recurs in a slightly different form in "The Work of Art," where he argues that the photographic and cinematic processes of the close-up and slow

> **" All knowledge takes the form of interpretation "**
> Walter Benjamin, *The Correspondence of Walter Benjamin, 1910–1940*

motion expose "entirely new structural formations of the subject" in a similar way to how psychoanalysts expose unconscious impulses.[4]

Affinities can also be found between "The Work of Art" and "The Author as Producer" (1934), which argues that under capitalism, publishing inherently participates in class conflict.[5] Thus the writer takes sides whether or not they are aware of it. Benjamin calls for the writer to side with the working classes (proletariat), and to combat the fascist tendencies inherent in the capitalist mode of production both through the content of their work and at the level of form. Writers should not see themselves as suppliers of works that fit into existing formal categories, but as *producers* of radical new forms. However, while "The Author as Producer" explores parallel ideas to "The Work of Art" (with regard to printing rather than photography/film), its hardline Marxist approach arguably renders it a less sophisticated or nuanced work.

Integration

Benjamin's concern in "The Work of Art" with the material conditions underlying artistic production, in turn aligns it with the themes of the *Arcades Project*, the book he spent the last thirteen years of his life writing.[6] The project focused on the early-nineteenth-century architectural form of Parisian passages (shopping arcades), which Benjamin saw as a symbol of capitalist delusion. Once the center of commerce, by the end of the nineteenth century the arcades had been made obsolete by department stores. Benjamin saw the now empty, derelict spaces of the arcades as symbolizing a culture in which today's prized possession is tomorrow's trash.

"The Work of Art" also bears some relation to "The Storyteller," an essay Benjamin was writing in the same period, which addressed a comparable erosion of the craft of storytelling as a consequence of the reproductive technologies of print.[7]

Finally, "The Work of Art" intersects with Benjamin's other work in its celebration of distraction. Benjamin spent the 1910s translating the work of the French poet Charles Baudelaire who, in "The Painter of Modern Life" (1863),* argued that modern urban life necessitated new modes of representation capable of capturing the constant flux and change of the capitalist city. For Baudelaire, the figure of the "*flâneur*"* (French for wanderer) embodies the qualities required of the modern poet: openness to absorbing (and writing about) the many shocks and stimuli of the city. Benjamin argued that in the twentieth century, such an approach was no longer possible: the possibility of *flânerie* was killed off by consumer capitalism. Twentieth-century capitalism's constant requirement of its citizens to take part in the processes of consumption and exchange renders distracted wandering unfeasible. Thus, in "The Work of Art," Benjamin identifies film as a new source for the measured distraction enjoyed by the nineteenth-century *flâneur*: not passive enjoyment, but rather a distanced and dispassionate engagement.[8]

Significance

While the argument of "The Work of Art" is fundamentally unique, Benjamin's unorthodox methodology here is characteristic of his work in general. His thinking consistently involves connecting various fragments from seemingly separate disciplines, such as art, architecture, film, photography, history, literature, philosophy, and politics. By grouping these fragments together within his essay, he constructs an innovative approach to thinking about art and politics, cultural production, and technological reproduction.

As the most widely read work of one of the most influential critics of the twentieth century, "The Work of Art" has proved to be a "game-changer" (albeit belatedly, many years after his death). Since the publication of the first English translation in the late 1960s, the essay has served for many people as a valuable introduction to Benjamin's corpus and remains a key reference point for the study of twentieth-century culture and modernity.

However, in more recent years, the essay has been less central to discussions of Benjamin's continued significance as a critic and theorist. This is largely owing to scholars' increased interest in other essays by Benjamin—most notably, "Theses on the Philosophy of History."[9] Benjamin's last completed work, this essay is a critique of historicism* (the attribution of meaning to historical circumstances, and the analysis of phenomena in relation to their historical context).

The diminishing centrality of "The Work of Art" in contemporary intellectual debate is also a consequence of the emergence in translation of various other material published after Benjamin's death.[10] Most notably, writings the Gestapo confiscated from Benjamin's last apartment in Paris were only transferred to the Walter Benjamin Archive in Berlin in 1996.[11] The two biographies of Benjamin, by Esther Leslie* in 2007 and by Howard Eiland* and Michael W. Thompson in 2013, have also contributed to new directions in Benjamin studies.[12] These writings have inspired a flood of commentary on lesser-researched aspects of Benjamin's work, as well as new translations. Thus, while "The Work of Art" remains important, it has arguably already fulfilled its original task—to open Benjamin's complex output to a seemingly endless process of interpretation.

NOTES

1 Walter Benjamin, "A Small History of Photography," in *One-Way Street and Other Writings*, trans. Edmund Jephcott, and Kingsley Shorter (London: Verso, 1999), 240–57.

2 Benjamin, "A Small History of Photography," 250.

3 Benjamin, "A Small History of Photography," 243.

4 Walter Benjamin, "The Work of Art in the Age of Mechanical Reproduction," in *Illuminations,* ed. Hannah Arendt (London: Pimlico, 1999), 229.

5 Walter Benjamin, "The Author as Producer," in *Understanding Brecht*, trans. Anna Bostock (London: Verso, 2003), 85–103.

6 Walter Benjamin, *Arcades Project,* ed. and trans. Howard Eiland and Kevin McLaughlin (Cambridge, MA: Belknap/Harvard University Press, 1999).

7 Walter Benjamin, "The Storyteller," in *Illuminations,* trans. Harry Zohn (London: Fontana, 1982), 83–109.

8 Benjamin, "The Work of Art," 233–34.

9 Walter Benjamin, "Theses on the Philosophy of History," in *Illuminations*, trans. by Harry Zohn (London: Fontana, 1982), 255–66. This essay has also been widely translated as "On the Concept of History."

10 Rolf J. Goebel, "Introduction: Benjamin's Actuality," in *A Companion to the Works of Walter Benjamin,* ed. Rolf J. Goebel (London: Camden House, 2009), 2.

11 Goebel, "Introduction: Benjamin's Actuality," 2.

12 Esther Leslie, *Walter Benjamin* (London: Reaktion, 2007); Howard Eiland and Michael W. Jennings, *Walter Benjamin: A Critical Life* (Cambridge, MA: Belknap Press/Harvard University Press, 2013).

THE FIRST RESPONSES

KEY POINTS

- The initial reception of "The Work of Art in the Age of Mechanical Reproduction" came before publication, from the leaders of the Institute for Social Research.

- Benjamin addressed the leaders' criticisms in a prolonged correspondence with Theodor Adorno.

- While some of the ideas in "The Work of Art" are flawed, the text is important to the study of twentieth-century art, technology, and politics.

Criticism

When "The Work of Art in the Age of Mechanical Reproduction" was first published in 1936 in the journal of the Institute for Social Research (in a French translation), it failed to stimulate the kind of ongoing debate about the relationship between aesthetics and politics that Benjamin had hoped.[1] It would be almost two decades before the essay was republished in Benjamin's native German, and three decades before its first appearance in an English translation, in 1968, that would help to ignite an explosion of interest in Benjamin's work.[2]

The first criticisms of the text came before its actual publication, from the scholars at the Institute of Social Research who had commissioned the piece, and with whom Benjamin was loosely affiliated. Adorno, in particular, engaged in an important discussion with Benjamin about the essay's merits and flaws.[3]

This discussion can be found in Benjamin's correspondence with Adorno, and particularly in a letter Adorno wrote in March 1936.[4] Here Adorno criticized Benjamin's essay for its overly optimistic view

> ❝[Adorno] asks, which art unmasks more effectively the barbaric circumstances that we inhabit? Both the highest, Kafka and Shoenberg, with their non-auratic, technically advanced and barbaric art without pleasure, and the lowest, Disney, Chaplin, and the art of the philistines, bear the stigmata *and* elements of change ... Mickey [Mouse's] magic magics away the urgency of social transformation.❞
>
> Esther Leslie, *Hollywood Flatlands, Critical Theory and the Avant-Garde*

of the revolutionary potential of film: "if anything can be said to possess an auratic character now, it is precisely film which does so, and to an extreme and highly suspect degree."[5] Adorno argued that it was "simple romanticization" to think that "a reactionary individual [could] be transformed into a member of the avant-garde"* just by watching a silent movie.[6] He opined that "the laughter of a cinema audience [was] anything but salutary and revolutionary"[7] and remained unconvinced by Benjamin's theory of distraction, "if only for the simple reason that in a communist society, work would be organized in such a way that human beings would no longer be so exhausted or so stupefied as to require distraction."[8]

Adorno also pointed out "how little" use films made of the optical effects Benjamin considered to hold so much radical potential. Most films, he commented, merely attempted to replicate reality.[9] He did, however, agree with Benjamin's assessment of Dada's techniques of shock as anticipating the shock effects of film.[10] Adorno's criticisms should also be understood as stemming from his own bias towards Benjamin's other work—he expressly stated in another letter: "I regard your work on the 'Arcades' as the center not merely of your own philosophy, but as the decisive philosophical word which must find utterance today."[11]

Responses

Although Benjamin acknowledged that Adorno's comments and criticisms were instructive, by the time he wrote the third version of the essay he had decided to maintain his position. In fact, he even removed his discussion of the fascist aspects of the violence in Mickey Mouse, which he had inserted into the essay's second version, and which anticipated Adorno's criticisms of Disney in "The Culture Industry."[12] To address Adorno's concerns, however, he supplemented the essay with lengthy footnotes. These footnotes, as leading Benjamin scholar Esther Leslie notes, betray Benjamin's ambivalent views towards cinema as both potentially liberating and potentially oppressive.[13] In Footnote Seven, for example, Benjamin explains how the development of sound film helped overcome the language barrier that was preventing international distribution and that was thus serving the nationalistic interests of fascism (which holds that viewing foreign works of art is unpatriotic). He argues that "viewed from the outside, the sound film promoted national interests, but seen from the inside it helped to internationalize film production even more than previously."[14]

Likewise, as Leslie notes, the epilogue of Benjamin's essay "reverse[s] the optimistic current—all the potential credited to art in the age of technology evaporated before the techno-mysticism and class-violence of the Nationalist Socialists."[15] In her words, Benjamin recognizes in this last section how "fascists mirrored mass society in representations without substance" by representing the masses formally (that is, depicting them on film), without "represent[ing] [them] politically in any meaningful way."[16] In tempering the optimism expressed in the other sections, Benjamin can be seen to address Adorno's concerns.

Conflict and Consensus

Because Benjamin died so soon after the completion of the essay's final draft, these disagreements with Adorno were never fully resolved—and scholars have, in fact, continued to debate them in the decades since. Likewise, while the essay did not generate the immediate response for which he hoped, it has since been recognized as a pioneering contribution to the study of political aesthetics—a discipline that examines the role of beauty and artistic representation in a political context, and which he, Adorno, Horkheimer, and others associated with the Frankfurt School, helped create.

The explosion of interest in Benjamin's essay in an English-language context since the nineteen seventies, after its translation into English in 1968, reflects a wider shift in what scholars deem worth studying. Benjamin's view that mass culture deserves to be examined as much as "High Culture,"* and that such examination should be purely negative in its assessment, anticipated later developments in literary studies and the social sciences. Like Benjamin's work, the field of Cultural Studies, for example, is premised on the idea that all cultural phenomena, not just those produced by and for the upper classes, are worthy of scholarly attention. Thus, while the commercial history of film in the post-World War II era makes Benjamin's revolutionary hopes for film appear naïve, its nuanced analyses make it a seminal artifact of 1930s critical thought, and an important predecessor to later film theory and cultural studies more broadly.[17] While its assessment of technology's long-term impact on art and culture under capitalism is arguably flawed, its attempt to understand these forms in the first place is important.

NOTES

1   Esther Leslie, "Revolutionary potential and Walter Benjamin: A postwar reception history," in *Critical Companion to Contemporary Marxism*, ed. Gregory Elliott and Jacques Bidet (Leiden: Brill, 2007), 549–66.

2   Leslie, "Revolutionary potential and Walter Benjamin," 549–66.

3   Adorno and Benjamin, *The Complete Correspondence: 1928–40*, 127–34.

4   Adorno and Benjamin, *The Complete Correspondence*, 127–34 (130).

5   Adorno and Benjamin, *The Complete Correspondence*, 132.

6   Adorno and Benjamin, *The Complete Correspondence*, 130.

7   Adorno and Benjamin, *The Complete Correspondence*, 130.

8   Adorno and Benjamin, *The Complete Correspondence*, 130.

9   Adorno and Benjamin, *The Complete Correspondence*, 131.

10 Adorno and Benjamin, *The Complete Correspondence*, 133.

11 Adorno and Benjamin, *The Complete Correspondence*, 85.

12 Esther Leslie, *Hollywood Flatlands, Critical Theory and the Avant-Garde* (London: Verso, 2002), 117–118. Benjamin's discussion of Disney can be found in *Walter Benjamin, The Work of Art in the Age of Its Technological Reproducibility and Other Writings on Media*, ed. Michael W. Jennings, Brigid Doherty, Thomas Y. Levin (Cambridge, MA: The Belknap Press, 2008), 318–38.

13 Leslie, *Hollywood Flatlands*, 117–118.

14 Walter Benjamin, "The Work of Art in the Age of Mechanical Reproduction," in *Illuminations,* ed. Hannah Arendt (London: Pimlico, 1999), 237.

15 Esther Leslie, *Walter Benjamin* (London: Reaktion, 2007),162.

16 Leslie, *Walter Benjamin*,163.

17 Angela McRobbie, "The *Passagenwerk* and the place of Walter Benjamin in cultural studies," *Cultural Studies* 6. 2 (1992): 147–69. Reprinted in *The Cultural Studies Reader,* ed. Simon During (London: Routledge, 1999), 77–96. See also Andrew Robinson, "Walter Benjamin and Critical Theory," *Ceasefire* (April 4, 2013). https://ceasefiremagazine.co.uk/in-theory-benjamin-1/. Accessed July 13, 2017.

MODULE 10
THE EVOLVING DEBATE

KEY POINTS

- "The Work of Art in the Age of Mechanical Reproduction" has a complex history as multiple versions of the essay exist, and its translation into English was delayed.

- Benjamin's essay is a pioneering work of political aesthetics and critical theory, and it has influenced art criticism and art history.

- Benjamin scholarship is roughly split between those who apply his ideas to the study of mass culture, and those who read them politically.

Uses and Problems

The story of the production and dissemination of Benjamin's essay is itself convoluted due both to its author's premature death and to the multiple versions and translations of it that exist. Benjamin wrote the original version in German in 1935. He then wrote a second version, which the Institute for Social Research modified, omitting the original's references to Marx, and translated into French before publishing it.[1] The final version, which Benjamin finished in 1939 and in which he re-introduced the previously omitted parts, was published in Germany in 1955 in an essay collection titled *Schriften*.[2]

The first English language edition of *Schriften*, edited by the noted German intellectual Hannah Arendt and translated by Harry Zohn as *Illuminations*, was published in 1968, featuring an introductory essay by Arendt that first appeared in *The New Yorker*.* This translation followed other appropriations of Benjamin's work by university students in

> **❝**Benjamin desires to ... release ... the potential of technology. Technology must be made to work for social transformation rather than enforcing the soporific dream state. The bourgeoisie sustains the dream state by conserving the relations of production in which technology is entwined ... The proletariat ... possesses the ability to revive collectively, through a realization of class-consciousness. **❞**
>
> Esther Leslie, *Walter Benjamin: Overpowering Conformism*

West Germany,* who exchanged pirate copies of his work during the student revolts of the late 1960s.[3] At a time of mass protests against establishment values (exemplified by the Paris uprisings* in May 1968), the Vietnam War,* racism, colonialism,* and social inequality, Benjamin's work gained new resonance.

Interest in "The Work of Art" fueled the translation into English of Benjamin's other work, previously either unpublished or only available in German. A first collection of his correspondence, edited by Adorno and published in Germany in 1978, was translated into English in 1994.[4] This was followed by an English translation of *The Arcades Project* in 1999, and of Adorno and Benjamin's complete correspondence in 2001.[5] Finally, two new translations of "The Work of Art" came out between 2008 and 2009: one, by J. A. Underwood, of the final version of the essay, and another, by Michael Jennings, of the second version, under the title "The Work of Art in The Age of Its Technological Reproducibility."[6] This latter title more accurately reflects the German original and more faithfully conveys Benjamin's wider interest in ideas related to *Technik*, a term that relates to both technique and technology—although Zohn's 1968 version remains the more frequently read.

Schools of Thought

Benjamin's essay has had a wide-ranging influence and it contributed directly to the very foundation of two schools of thought. Together with Max Horkheimer, Theodor Adorno, Erich Fromm* and Herbert Marcuse,* Benjamin helped establish the discipline of critical theory. In his essay "Traditional and Critical theory" (1937),* Horkheimer states that a theory is critical if it seeks to "liberate human beings from the circumstances that enslave them."[7] In contrast to the "traditional" methods of natural scientists, who merely seek to explain phenomena, critical theory aims to both investigate and challenge the status quo— and particularly capitalism's influence on power structures. As a text that explores technological reproduction in order to forge ways of opposing dominant modes of thinking, Benjamin's essay can be seen as among the very first works of critical theory.

Benjamin and his Frankfurt School colleagues likewise laid the groundwork for political aesthetics. Benjamin's famous statements in the epilogue of "The Work of Art," that "The logical result of Fascism is the introduction of aesthetics into political life" and that "[a]ll efforts to render politics aesthetic culminate in one thing: war,"[8] are among the foundational concepts of political aesthetics, which is likewise concerned with how political ideas and movements expressed and represented in culture serve to advance ideological shifts or to uphold oppressive regimes.

Within art history and criticism, writer and art critic John Berger (1926–2017) famously incorporated ideas from Benjamin's essay into his 1970s television series *Ways of Seeing.** The show was subsequently adapted as a popular introductory book on art history that is now widely used on university syllabi.[9] In the first chapter of the book of *Ways of Seeing*, Berger explains that the reverence individuals are encouraged to feel towards artworks as unique, unchanging objects is related to broader efforts to keep the dominant class in place. When a work of art becomes technically reproducible another set of assumptions (or what he calls "mystifications") threaten to set in: these need to be challenged. At the end of the chapter he acknowledges his intellectual debt to Benjamin's essay.[10]

In Current Scholarship

Crudely summarized, Benjamin scholarship since the 1970s can be split into two strands. First, there are those within the US strand of cultural studies, which in contrast to its UK counterpart has, since the mid-1980s, tended to examine mass culture apolitically.[11] For many years, US cultural studies tended to approach Benjamin as a critic on the margins of academia—since Benjamin did not hold an academic post—to be praised for his focus on everyday phenomena and his appreciation of film and photography as worthy of attention.[12] Such scholarship largely ignored the political dimensions of Benjamin's work, and is arguably symptomatic of the broader decline in the popularity of critical theory in US academia during the 1980s and 1990s that resulted from the dominance of neoliberal* ideology fueled by the Reagan* and Bush* administrations, and the perceived triumph of capitalism over communism* after the collapse of the Soviet Union* in 1991. In the wake of communism's defeat, and at a time of relative economic prosperity, there appeared to be little need to examine anti-capitalist writing—a view that the US novelist Jonathan Franzen* parodies in his 2001 novel, *The Corrections*, where the English professor protagonist sells off all of his Frankfurt School books (including Benjamin's) for pennies.[13]

These de-politicized applications of Benjamin's work were anticipated by the Marxist literary critic* Terry Eagleton* in his 1981 study, *Walter Benjamin; or, Towards a Revolutionary Criticism* (1981), where he openly stated his aim to "get to Benjamin before the opposition does."[14] The second strand of Benjamin scholarship echoes Eagleton in its efforts to oppose the dilution of Benjamin's radicalism. From the perspective of these scholars, Benjamin's essay is first and foremost the work of an exiled German Jew involved in opposing capitalism, fascism, and war. Only from this basis does it become possible to use the text in ways that illuminate our own cultural, historical, political, and social contexts. Thus, in *Walter Benjamin: Against Conformism* (2000), one of the first books in English to reclaim Benjamin's politics, Esther Leslie argues that Benjamin's work as a whole should be understood as actively engaging with the prospect of a "military atrocity … intensified by technological means."[15]

NOTES

1   Esther Leslie, "The Work of Art in the Age of Unbearable Capitulation," in *Walter Benjamin: Overpowering Conformism* (London: Reaktion, 2000), 131.

2   Walter Benjamin, *Schriften* (Frankfurt am Main: Suhrkamp Verlag, 1955).

3   Esther Leslie, *Walter Benjamin* (London: Reaktion, 2007), 227.

4   Walter Benjamin, *Arcades Project,* ed. and trans. Howard Eiland and Kevin McLaughlin (Cambridge, MA: Belknap/Harvard University Press, 1999).

5   Theodor W. Adorno and Walter Benjamin, *The Complete Correspondence: 1928–40*, trans. Nicholas Walker (Cambridge: Polity, 1999).

6   Walter Benjamin, "The Work of Art in the Age of Mechanical Reproduction," in *One-Way Street and Other Writings,* ed. Amit Chaudhuri and trans. J.A. Underwood (London and New York: Penguin, 2008), 228–59; "The Work of Art in the Age of its Technological Reproducibility" in *The Work of Art in the Age of Its Technological Reproducibility and Other Writings on Media*, ed. Michael W. Jennings, Brigid Doherty, Thomas Y. Levin (Cambridge, MA: Belknap/Harvard University Press, 2008).

7   Max Horkheimer, "Traditional and Critical Theory" (1937), in *Selected Essays* (London and New York: Continuum, 1982), 188–244 (244).

8   Benjamin, "The Work of Art," 234.

9   John Berger, *Ways of Seeing* (London: Penguin, 1977), 34.

10   Berger, *Ways of Seeing,* 34.

11 John Clarke, "Cultural Studies: a British inheritance," in *New Times and Old Enemies: Essays on Cultural Studies and America* (New York: HarperCollins, 1991); Robert W. McChesney, "Whatever happened to cultural studies?" in *American Cultural Studies,* ed. Catherine A. Warren and Mary Douglas Vavrus (Chicago: University of Illinois Press, 2002), 76–93; Cary Nelson, "Always Already Cultural Studies" in *English Studies/Cultural Studies: Institutionalizing Dissent,* ed. Isaiah Smithson and Nancy Ruff (Chicago: University of Illinois Press, 1994), 191–206.

12 For an example of this critique, see Janet Wolff, "Memoirs and Micrologies: Walter Benjamin, feminism, and cultural analysis" in *Walter Benjamin: Critical Interventions in Cultural Theory. Vol III: Appropriations*, ed. Peter Osborne (London: Routledge, 2005), 319–33.

13 Jonathan Franzen, *The Corrections* (London: Fourth Estate, 2001), 106.

14 Terry Eagleton, *Walter Benjamin; or, Towards a Revolutionary Criticism* (London: Verso, 1981), ii.

15 Leslie, "The Work of Art in the Age of Unbearable Capitulation," 1.

IMPACT AND INFLUENCE TODAY

KEY POINTS

- "The Work of Art in the Age of Mechanical Reproduction" remains a reference point for scholars interested in twentieth-century art, culture, technology, and politics.

- Benjamin scholars have recently critiqued Benjamin studies' own complicity in downplaying the more radical aspects of Benjamin's work.

- Scholars also debate the ethical implications of the depoliticized portrayal of Benjamin in undergraduate guides to his work.

Position

"The Work of Art in the Age of Mechanical Reproduction" is still considered a pioneering work of scholarship, and it continues to be anthologized, taught in university classrooms, and referenced in academic scholarship. This is partly because the essay anticipated or provided the groundwork for contemporary discussions about the relationship between art, technology, and politics. It is also because Benjamin's ideas help shed light on the work of his artist and writer contemporaries. "The Work of Art" surfaces in countless books on early-twentieth-century art, cinema, photography, and literature. For example, the essays in Pamela Caughie's edited collection, *Virginia Woolf in the Age of Mechanical Reproduction* (2000), apply Benjamin's ideas to highlight the significance of technological reproducibility in the life and fiction of British author Virginia Woolf.*[1] Likewise, Lara Feigel's *Literature, Cinema, and Politics 1930–1945: Reading Between the Frames* (2010), adopts Benjamin's ideas to examine the relationship

66 The mere existence of a 'Benjamin industry' is not in itself extraordinary. The commodification* of various intellectuals is a common capitalist phenomenon, especially in the age of mass media and broader access to education, as witness by the popularity of James Joyce fridge magnet dolls or Sigmund Freud slippers. 99

Udi E. Greenberg, "The Politics of the Walter Benjamin Industry"

between film and literature in the immediate run-up to, and during, World War II.[2]

Beyond these historical studies, Benjamin's essay is cited in discussions concerning digital technology.[3] Rolf Goebel, for example, notes that Benjamin's view of the radical potential of new technologies to disrupt the status quo is vindicated by "virtual reality scenarios that can be received all over the world" and in which "the aura of authenticity and uniqueness—both with respect to works of art and topographic sites—seems increasingly to disappear."[4]

These media have the "salutary" effect of "demystify[ing] the terrifying or intriguing strangeness of faraway lands"—making us more likely to empathize with those different from us, and providing a corrective to authoritarian* rulers' efforts to pit nations against each other.[5] At the same time, digital media have the capacity to endow specific images of political unrest or protest with universal qualities, rendering them emblems of pro-democratic movements globally.[6] "In contrast to Benjamin's identification of political aura with Fascism, this kind of aestheticizing of politics by the mass media is now coded as democratic self-articulation and anti-authoritarian defiance."[7]

Interaction

One of the recurring questions debated by Benjamin scholars today regards whether assuming his work to be universally applicable in fact goes against its very ethos, which sought to examine cultural phenomena within their specific historical context. A second relates to whether meaningful Benjamin scholarship is possible at a time when universities themselves are increasingly under pressure to discourage radical thinking. A third regards the need to critically examine the history of Benjamin scholarship *itself*, and to acknowledge that it, too, has been shaped by capitalist ideology—and that there is something questionable about capitalizing (making money) on the ideas of someone so vehemently opposed to capitalist consumer culture.

In a keynote address at the first Congress of the International Walter Benjamin Association in 1997, Benjamin scholar Susan Buck-Morss commented on what she saw to be the "irony" of the very existence of a Walter Benjamin conference, when the writer himself was ostracized by academia for his views.[8] She further argued that meaningful Benjamin scholarship must seek to retain Benjamin's view that "What we do, or do not do, creates the present; what we know, or do not know, constructs the past. These two tasks are inextricably connected in that how we construct the past determines how we understand the present course." Morss's "we" referred to Benjamin scholars themselves, whom she noted have downplayed aspects of "The Work of Art," such as its exploration of Soviet socialist art.

The view that the history of Benjamin scholarship itself requires study is echoed by Esther Leslie in her many articles and books on Benjamin, where she repeatedly calls for more recognition of his radical politics, and, most recently, in *Guardian* journalist Stuart Jeffries's *Grand Hotel Abyss: The Lives of the Frankfurt School* (2016), which traces the evolution of the Institute for Social Research as well as the changing reception and application of its scholars' ideas that has resulted from broader shifts in global politics.[9]

The Continuing Debate

The question about how Benjamin's ideas are used is ultimately an ethical* one. In the broadest terms, ethics are the moral principles that guide our behavior, based on our understanding of what is right and what is wrong. In this case, the question remains whether it is possible to use Benjamin's ideas productively, and in the spirit that he championed, when the very environments in which this occurs (the university classroom, the publishing industry, the conference circuit) are caught up with the capitalist enterprises he opposed. For example, is the ubiquitous presence of Benjamin's work in art museum book stores, or Buzzfeed's* dissemination of Benjamin memes a good thing—helping disseminate his ideas further—or a sign that he has been co-opted?[10]

Scholar Udi E. Greenberg examines these questions in his 2008 essay, "The Politics of the Walter Benjamin Industry," where he traces the assimilation of Benjamin's ideas into popular culture (from experimental musician and artist Laurie Anderson's 1987 film short *What Do You Mean We?* to Benjamin's more recent depiction in the popular 2005 opera *Shadowtime*) before examining academia's own ambiguous relationship to his ideas.[11] According to Greenberg, "Over the last two decades [1988–2008], the German-Jewish thinker was torn from his political context, became a source of personal and ideological identification, and was then returned to the public as a form of socialization."[12] Greenberg goes on to analyze Benjamin's idealized portrayal in publications such as the comic book *Benjamin for Beginners* (2001) and American writer Jay Parini's* novel *Benjamin's Crossing* (1996), to show how "the life and work of the radical thinker were narrated in conservative formulae, producing 'Benjamin' as the signifier not of political subversion, but of social disengagement and disorientation."[13]

NOTES

1 Pamela Caughie, *Virginia Woolf in the Age of Mechanical Reproduction* (London: Routledge, 2000).

2 Lara Feigel, *Literature, Cinema, and Politics 1930–1945: Reading Between the Frames* (Edinburgh University Press, 2010).

3 Freya Schiwy and Alessandro Fornazzari, eds. *Digital Media, Cultural Production and Speculative Capitalism* (London: Routledge, 2013); Jaeho Kang's *Walter Benjamin and the Media: The Spectacle of Modernity* (Cambridge: Polity Press, 2014); Laura J. Shepherd and Caitlin Hamilton, eds. *Understanding Popular Culture and World Politics in the Digital Age* (London: Routledge, 2016).

4 Rolf Goebel, "Introduction: Benjamin's Actuality," in *A Companion to the Works of Walter Benjamin,* ed. Rolf Goebel (London: Camden House, 2009), 1–22.

5 Goebel, 11.

6 Goebel, 11.

7 Goebel, 11.

8 Susan Buck-Morss, "Anti-Stalinist Art: Benjamin, Shostakovich, and the End of the Story," Keynote lecture of the first Congress of the International Walter Benjamin Association, Amsterdam, July 1997. Published as "Revolutionary Time: The Vanguard and the Avant-Garde" in *Benjamin Studies, Studien 1,* ed. Helga Geyer Ryan (Amsterdam: Rodopi, 2002). http://susanbuckmorss.info/text/antistalinist-art/ Accessed July 13, 2017.

9 Stuart Jeffries, *Grand Hotel Abyss: The Lives of the Frankfurt School* (London: Verso, 2016).

10 Matt Ortile, "11 Wonderful Illuminating Quotes from Walter Benjamin: Get ready for some *Illuminations* in Honor of His 122nd Birthday Today!" *Buzzfeed* (July 15, 2014), accessed June 30, 2017. https://www.buzzfeed.com/mattortile/work-of-art-in-the-age-of-social-discovery?utm_term=.vb8mqkAAj#.shK5pgyyD.

11 Udi E. Greenberg, "The Politics of the Walter Benjamin Industry," *Theory, Culture & Society* 25, no. 3 (2008): 53–68, accessed June 28, 2017. http://journals.sagepub.com.libproxy.ucl.ac.uk/doi/pdf/10.1177/0263276408090657. DOI: 10.1177/0263276408090657.

12 Greenberg, 61.

13 Greenberg, 68.

WHERE NEXT?

KEY POINTS

- Like its reception to date, future applications of "The Work of Art in the Age of Mechanical Reproduction" will inevitably be shaped by the broader political climate.

- Skepticism of neoliberalism and the rise of the far right in Europe and the US will likely fuel Benjamin scholarship in the near future.

- "The Work of Art" is a key reference for anyone interested in better understanding the relationship between art, technology, and politics.

Potential

The enduring influence of Walter Benjamin's essay across the humanities and social sciences reflects both the essay's originality and acuity and its relevance for understanding the seismic shifts in western—if not global—politics since it was written. What's more, the broader political environment, which has shaped the course of the essay's reception in the near-century since its publication, will also, in all likelihood, affect the direction of Benjamin scholarship in future. Thus, just as the neoliberal political climate of the 1980s and 1990s generated more conservative readings of Benjamin among scholars in English-speaking countries, there are some indications now that the tide has turned towards more radical analyses. For one thing, Benjamin's criticisms of capitalism chime with the questioning of free market ideology (also known as neoliberalism) manifest in much journalism and academic scholarship in the wake of the 2007–2008 global financial crisis,* some of which makes explicit reference to his

> ❝ Mass reproduction is aided especially by the reproduction of masses. In big parades and monster rallies, in sports events, and in war, all of which nowadays are captured by camera … the masses are brought face to face with themselves. This process … is intimately connected with the development of the techniques of reproduction and photography. ❞
>
> Walter Benjamin, "The Work of Art in the Age of Mechanical Reproduction"

work.[1] For another, Benjamin's analysis of fascism's manipulation of public opinion has evident applications for understanding the rise of far-right movements in Europe and the US, which has been frequently compared to that of the 1930s.[2]

Finally, Benjamin's work has instigated interest outside of academia since 2015, when Donald Trump first announced his candidacy for the US presidency. A slew of articles during and in the immediate aftermath of the US presidential election cited Benjamin, Adorno, and Horkheimer as key reference points for understanding Trump's theatrics, which they they claimed resembled Hitler's deft manipulations of the media.[3]

Each of these events—the global financial crisis and ensuing policy of austerity,* which increased social inequality in much of Europe and the US; the ensuing rise of the far-right, and, in Greece and Spain, the far-left; and the US election—have prompted an unprecedented public interest in Benjamin's ideas.

Future Directions

In light of the political shifts just described, Benjamin's epilogue on war and aesthetics is especially ripe for re-consideration. Here, Benjamin explained how fascism "attempts to organize the newly created proletarian masses without affecting the property structure which the masses strive to eliminate."[4]

Fascism achieves this by creating a cult around its leaders, which then allows it to justify violence and the further production of "ritual values" (values associated with the dictator's regimes, in this case). Not only traditional art forms, but cinema and other forms of mass media can be used for such manipulative purposes. From here, Benjamin argues that only war "makes it possible to mobilize all of today's technical resources while maintaining the property system."[5] Art and technology can help maintain a seemingly unchangeable political position in which the majority of people are kept subordinate to a minority with a vested interest.

While an in-depth application of Benjamin's concept of art, technology, and war to twenty-first century politics remains to be written, scholars and journalists have certainly skirted the edges of the topic through analyses of Trump's use of spectacle to gain and manipulate power.[6] In *The Citizen Marketer: Promoting Political Opinion in the Social Media Age* (2017), for example, Joel Penney applies Benjamin's discussion of the aestheticization of politics to an analysis of Trump's campaign tactics, which included paying people to attend the rally where he announced his candidacy.[7] Mark Andrejevic,* in turn, applies Benjamin's ideas to a discussion of Trump's media persona and the demagoguery* that characterized his campaign.[8] Anthropologists Donna M. Goldstein and Kira Hall have likewise used Walter Benjamin's essay, and the ideas of Benjamin scholar Susan Buck-Morss, to examine Trump's "spectacle of governing."[9]

Beyond these issues, the revolutionary energies that Benjamin's essay identifies are likely to be used to examine the capture and sharing of everyday experience via mobile phones and other audiovisual recording devices. In one aside in his essay, Benjamin already addresses a similar point when registering that with the rise of letters to the editor and other forms of audience engagement at the end of the nineteenth century and the beginning of the twentieth century, "an increasing number of readers became writers."[10]

In fact, in a passage that predates the internet by almost six decades, Benjamin describes a situation very close to at least one geographical section of the contemporary world of online bloggers: "today there is hardly a gainfully employed European who could not, in principle, find an opportunity to publish somewhere or other comments on his work, grievances, documentary reports, or that sort of thing."[11]

Summary

Over the successive decades since its composition, the revolutionary optimism that Benjamin expressed in "The Work of Art in the Age of Mechanical Reproduction" has spectacularly failed to instigate revolutionary change. Film has proved to be a far more reactionary medium than Benjamin had hoped, while for many years scholars approached the essay itself in the exact terms Benjamin sought to oppose, focusing on the changes he identified in art's reception rather than on their political ramifications. From this perspective, one could argue that the essay was co-opted, despite Benjamin's best intentions, not for fascist purposes, but certainly to conservative ends—that is, by critics with no interest in changing the status quo.

Despite these drawbacks, however, "The Work of Art" remains a pivotal text in art history and literary studies, and a touchstone for radical art criticism today. What is more, it effectively laid the groundwork for the fields of cultural studies, media studies, and political aesthetics, enabling the emergence of entirely new ways of examining phenomena as varied as television, celebrity culture, user-generated content,* and memes.* Benjamin's concepts of the withered aura, cult value, and ritual value continue to be used by art historians, while his identification of the aestheticization of politics in the age of radio, film, and photography anticipated subsequent debates around politics in the age of television, social media, and reality shows.

For all of these reasons, "The Work of Art" still has much to teach us, both in terms of how we view art and experience new media, and in terms of art and new media's capacity to change our worldview—for better or for worse.

NOTES

1   Roger Berkowitz and Taun N. Toay, eds. *The Intellectual Origins of the Global Financial Crisis* (New York: Fordham University Press, 2013), 164–65; Philip Mirowski, *Never Let a Serious Crisis Go to Waste: How Neoliberalism Survived the Financial Meltdown* (London: Verso, 2013), 84, 100. Miriam Meissner, *Narrating the Global Financial Crisis: Urban Imaginaries and the Politics of Myth* (New York and Basingstoke: Palgrave, 2017), 21; 40–45.

2   For a sense of these discussions, see: John Palmer, "The rise of the far right parties across Europe is a chilling echo of the 1930s," *Guardian* (November 15, 2013), accessed June 30, 2017. https://www.theguardian.com/commentisfree/2013/nov/15/far-right-threat-europe-integration, Peter Foster, "The rise of the far-right in Europe is not a false alarm," *Telegraph* (May 19, 2016), accessed June 30, 2017. http://www.telegraph.co.uk/news/2016/05/19/the-rise-of-the-far-right-in-europe-is-not-a-false-alarm/. Mark Mardell, "Fascism, the 1930s, and the 21st century," *BBC News* (December 20, 2016), accessed June 30, 2017. http://www.bbc.co.uk/news/uk-politics-38317787. "No, this isn't the 1930s—but yes, this is fascism" *Faculty of History, University of Oxford* (November 16, 2016), accessed June 30, 2017. http://www.history.ox.ac.uk/article/no-isnt-1930s-yes-fascism.

3   Alexander Binnet, "Donald Trump and the Aesthetics of Fascism: What a 20th-century Marxist art critic can teach us about a very 21st-century candidate," *In These Times* (January 28, 2016), accessed June 28, 2017. http://inthesetimes.com/article/18807/donald-trump-and-the-aesthetics-of-fascism. Thomas Dumm, "Degraded fascism, nihilism, and Donald Trump," *Contemporary Condition* (September 2015), accessed June 28, 2017. http://contemporarycondition.blogspot.co.uk/2015/09/degraded-fascism-nihilism-and-donald.html.

3   Alex Ross, "The Frankfurt School knew Trump was Coming," *New Yorker* (December 5, 2016), accessed June 28, 2017. http://www.newyorker.com/culture/cultural-comment/the-frankfurt-school-knew-trump-was-coming.

4   Walter Benjamin, "The Work of Art in the Age of Mechanical Reproduction," in *Illuminations,* ed. Hannah Arendt (London: Pimlico, 1999), 234.

5   Benjamin, "The Work of Art," 234.

6   See, for example David Denby, "The Plot Against America: Trump's Rhetoric," *New Yorker* (December 15, 2015), accessed June 30, 2017. http://www.newyorker.com/culture/cultural-comment/plot-america-donald-trumps-rhetoric. Oliver Jones, *Donald Trump: The Rhetoric* (London: Eyeware Publishing, 2016). Ronald Brownstein, "Trump's rhetoric of white nostalgia," *The Atlantic* (June 2, 2016), accessed June 30, 2017. "https://www.theatlantic.com/politics/archive/2016/06/trumps-rhetoric-of-white-nostalgia/485192/. Sam Leith, "Trump's rhetoric: a triumph of inarticulacy," *Guardian* (January 13, 2017), accessed June 30, 2017. https://www.theguardian.com/us-news/2017/jan/13/donald-trumps-rhetoric-how-being-inarticulate-is-seen-as-authentic.

7   Joel Penney, *Citizen Marketer: Promoting Political Opinion in the Social Media Age* (Oxford: Oxford University Press, 2017), 113.

8   Mark Andrejevic, "The *Jouissance* of Trump," *Television and New Media* 17, no. 7 (2016): 651–55.

9   Donna M. Goldstein and Kira Hall, "Postelection surrealism and nostalgic racism in the hands of Donald Trump," *HAU: Journal of Ethnographic Theory* 7, no. 1 (2017): http://dx.doi.org/10.14318/hau7.1.026.

10 Benjamin, "The Work of Art," 225.

11 Benjamin, "The Work of Art," 225.

GLOSSARY OF TERMS

Aestheticization of politics: an expression coined by Benjamin (with the help of Bertolt Brecht) to refer to fascist leaders' use of spectacular displays to inspire allegiance to the state and draw attention away from the oppressive realities of their policies. This concept is central to Benjamin's argument in "The Work of Art."

Anti-Semitism: prejudice, hostility, or discrimination towards Jewish people, which can range from the belief in entrenched stereotypes (e.g. "all Jewish people are tight with money") and use of prejudicial expressions (e.g. "to Jew someone down" in reference to haggling for a lower price) to the committing of acts of violence and implementation of discriminatory laws.

Arcades Project, The **(1927–):** Benjamin's last, and unfinished, project, which examined the Paris arcades as symbols of nineteenth-century capitalist modernity.

Art criticism: the critique of art works, whether in an academic context or in the public arena (for example, for newspapers or magazines). Benjamin's essay is both a work of art criticism and a criticism of traditional art criticism.

"Art for Art's Sake": a mode of viewing art that emerged in France in the nineteenth century, according to which art works have an inherent, unchanging value that is entirely separate to their moral function or practical use. Benjamin's essay is a critique of this approach and argues that it can all too easily be co-opted for fascist purposes.

Art history: the academic study of the history and development of visual art works including painting and sculpture. Benjamin's essay seeks to trace an alternative art history that takes into account the material conditions of art production.

Aura: an elusive term Benjamin coins in "The Work of Art" to denote the originality of a work of art, its separation from and superiority to everyday life, and its capacity to induce reverence in its viewers. The aura is connected to the artwork's cult value and ritualistic role—that is, its historical centrality to rituals related to the church, the monarchy, or ancient rites.

Austerity: in economics, the conditions created by government cuts to expenditure on public services (e.g. welfare, public housing, health services).

"The Author as Producer": an essay by Walter Benjamin that outlines ideas he later expanded upon in "The Work of Art." In particular, he argues that there can be no such thing as autonomous or apolitical art. The essay is much more orthodox in its Marxist stance than "The Work of Art" or his later work.

Authoritarianism: a form of government requiring obedience to authority at the expense of personal liberties. Fascism is a violent, nationalist form of authoritarianism. References to fascism were changed to "authoritarianism" in the first version of Benjamin's essay.

Autonomous/autonomy: independent/independence; a term Benjamin uses to refer to the art for art's sake movement's insistence on art's independence/separation from everyday affairs.

Avant-garde (see European Avant-garde)

Buzzfeed: a US digital media company based in New York City that specializes in social news and entertainment, with a particular focus on digital media and technology.

Capitalism: an economic system in which individuals and groups who privately own goods and services control industry and trade, rather than the state. The forum in which trade takes place is the marketplace.

Capitalistic mode of production: a system involving private (rather than state) ownership of the means of production, which allows the owners of the means of production (*bourgeoisie*) to accumulate wealth by extracting the surplus value (profit margin) of what their employees (*proletariat*) make/sell.

***Charles Baudelaire, Tableaux Parisiens* (1923):** Walter Benjamin's German translation of French poet Charles Baudelaire's (1821–67) poetry collection, *Tableaux Parisiens*. Baudelaire had a profound influence on Benjamin and re-appears in many of his essays, and in his unfinished work, *The Arcades Project* (1927–).

Cold War (1947–1991): a period of intense military and political tension following World War II between Western powers (the United States and its NATO allies) and Eastern powers including the Soviet Union, East Germany and China. It formally ended in 1991 with the collapse of the Soviet Union.

Colonialism: refers to the rule of one country by another, involving unequal power relations between the ruler (colonist) and ruled (colony), and the exploitation of the colony's resources to strengthen the economy of the colonizers' home country.

Collage: a work of visual art composed of fragments of mixed media (newspaper clippings, magazine cut-outs, etc.) that often do not appear related. Collage emerged as an artistic form in the early twentieth century; its first practitioners sought to blur the boundary between art and everyday life and to challenge capitalism.

Commodification: the transformation of something into a commodity (something that can be sold or profited from). Benjamin's work examines how how commodities can be stripped of their moneymaking status and used to resist capitalism.

Commodity fetishism: the transformation of social relations under capitalism into transactions. According to Marx, capitalism transforms social relations between human beings into economic relations between objects. Benjamin was interested in how objects could be stripped of their money-making status and used for radical purposes.

Communism: an economic system originally proposed by Karl Marx, in which the means of production (e.g. natural resources, factories, manufacturing equipment) are collectively owned. Marx envisioned a communist society as having no social classes. Benjamin's essay proposes a theory of art based on communist ideals to counter fascism's aestheticization of politics.

"The Conquest of Ubiquity" (1928): essay by French writer Paul Valéry (1871–1945) about the effects of technology on everyday life, in which he also speculates about future technological developments. Benjamin quotes Valéry in his own essay.

Co-option: the appropriation or assimilation of ideas or work of a smaller, usually weaker, group or individual. Benjamin's essay seeks to formulate a theory of art that will not be co-opted for fascist purposes.

Critical theory: a discipline founded by Benjamin and his fellow Frankfurt School scholars in the 1930s, and which aimed to go beyond the remit of "traditional theory" of explaining phenomena to actively find ways of rectifying social ills, such as class inequality and the abuse of power.

Cultural studies: an academic field of study characterized by a multidisciplinary approach (derived from the social sciences and the humanities) to the study of contemporary (especially mass) culture (Oxford English Dictionary).

"The Culture Industry": an essay by Max Horkheimer and Theodor Adorno that argues that mass culture under capitalism is an industry whose aim is to keep the masses pacified and accepting of the status quo.

Dada: a literary and artistic movement at the beginning of the twentieth century that broke with convention in order to create works designed to startle, shock, and scandalize the public. The movement was partly a response to the horrors of World War I, and partly an effort to challenge the commercialization of art and the encroachment of capitalism on all aspects of everyday life—all of which greatly influenced Walter Benjamin.

Demagoguery: a manipulative form of persuasion based on appealing to people's feelings, prejudices, and base instincts rather than convincing them through logic. The form is usually associated with political dictators and dishonest politicians.

Depoliticize/depoliticization: the removal of politics from an activity or cultural phenomenon; for example, a depoliticized analysis of a text ignores its political dimensions including any political references within the text itself, focusing on other elements.

Distraction: that which prevents one from concentrating on something else; the state of being unable to concentrate. Frankfurt School scholars were interested in the distracting effect of mass culture under capitalism; Benjamin argued that it was potentially a good thing.

Ethics: the moral principles (distinction between what is right and what is wrong) that guide our behavior; the study of how such moral principles are established or followed.

European avant-garde: generally refers to radical or countercultural European art and literature produced between 1910 and World War II, including movements such as Cubism, Dada, Surrealism, and Futurism. These movements all shared a concern with breaking with traditional conventions in art.

Fascism: any right-wing authoritarian regime; Walter Benjamin was concerned specifically with its organization and evolution in Europe during his lifetime, and the degree to which it relied on propaganda, the aestheticization of military power (making military power "beautiful"), and nostalgic motifs (making people long for the past).

Flâneur: a direct translation of the French term for wandering, the word was first used by Charles Baudelaire to define the experience of urban walking in modernity. Benjamin appropriated it in his readings of the nineteenth-century city, arguing that with the supplanting of the Paris arcades with department stores, and the introduction of the standard working day, the potential for true *flânerie* also died.

Frankfurt School: a term used to refer to several important leftist philosophers and theorists—prolific and influential scholars based at the University of Frankfurt am Main during the 1920s and 1930s, such as the German philosophers Max Horkheimer (1895–1973) and Theodore W. Adorno (1903–1969), who were colleagues of Walter Benjamin.

Futurism: an experimental art movement that emerged in Italy at the beginning of the twentieth century, and which championed speed, technology, and war, which its leaders said would allow Italy to become a leading European power. The movement was closely associated with Benito Mussolini's fascist party.

Genre: from the French word for "type," this is a term used to denote the category of an artwork, e.g. "mystery," "comedy," "tragedy," "romance," "western," etc. Critics often examine artworks in relation to other works from the same genre, and consider whether an artwork follows or challenges the conventions of its genre.

Gestapo: Nazi Germany and occupied Europe's official secret police (the word is an abbreviation of *Geheime Staatspolizei*, the German for "Secret State Police." The Gestapo was formed in 1933 and dissolved in May 1945, with Germany's surrender.

Global financial crisis of 2007–2008: a financial crisis that started in the United States and spread through much of Europe, and that experts have termed the worst economic upheaval since the depression of the 1930s. Because it was instigated by crises in the subprime mortgage market (involving the sale of loans to people who will have trouble repaying them) and in the banking sector, both of which were caused by lax regulations, one effect of has been a renewed criticism of free market capitalism.

Great Depression: an economic downturn that affected the US and Europe that began with a stock-market crash in 1929, continued for much of the 1930s, and did not officially end until after World War II. The success of the nationalist and xenophobic strands of fascism during this period have been attributed to the dire poverty experienced by people at this time, which created a heightened receptiveness to blaming minorities and Jews for wider systemic problems.

High culture: a term used to denote works of art produced for and often by the elite, and considered exclusive, rare, and superior to mass culture, which by definition is intended for large audiences.

Historicism: broadly speaking, the theory that social events and phenomena are determined by history. Benjamin was critical of this view, arguing that any meaningful understanding of past events must take into consideration the material (socio-economic) conditions that caused them.

Institute for Social Research: together with the University of Frankfurt am Main, this was the center of German intellectual thought in the first half of the twentieth century. From 1930, under the directorship of Max Horkheimer (1895–1973), it was heavily involved in research combining Marxist philosophy and Freudian psychoanalysis. Those associated with the Institute are also known as the "Frankfurt School."

Jewish mysticism: the academic study of different forms of mysticism throughout Jewish history. Scholars generally attribute the origins of the discipline to the writings of Walter Benjamin's friend and colleague Gershom Scholem (1897–1982), starting with Scholem's *Major Trends in Jewish Mysticism* (1941).

Late Roman Art Industry **(1905):** a book by art historian Alois Riegl (1858–1905), that sought to understand the art of the Late Roman period by studying both grandiose monuments and everyday objects like belt buckles. This approach, which involved the assumption that objects do not have to be valuable to be worth studying, was a key inspiration for Walter Benjamin.

Literary studies: the study, interpretation, and evaluation of literary works, including the assessment of their formal characteristics, their reflection or questioning of cultural norms, and/or their socio-political and historical influence.

Marxism (see Western Marxism)

Marxist literary criticism: the application of Marxist ideas to the analysis of literary texts, generally involving an emphasis on the economic conditions that produced the text, which the text reflects in its depiction of socio-economic relations.

Mass culture: a term used to describe the values and ideas that arise from a common/collective exposure to the same media (be these news sources, art, music, or literature). The term "mass" refers to the idea that the culture is being generated by the masses themselves rather than being imposed on them from above—an idea that Benjamin explores in his essay.

Meme: in the broadest terms, an idea, belief or expression that spreads rapidly throughout culture. More commonly, the term is used in reference to (usually humorous) online images, videos and pieces of text that are copied, modified, and disseminated across the Internet.

Montage: the literary and cinematic counterpart of collage;★ a composite whole made of fragments, images, text, or other media. In film, it refers to the splicing, alteration, or editing of images. In literature, it refers to the splicing of unrelated texts.

Nationalism: the belief that one's nation is superior to others and that allegiance to the nation should come above all other concerns; an extreme form of patriotism. Nationalism was a central component of the fascist movements that rose to power during Benjamin's time.

National Socialist German Workers' Party: also known as the Nazi party; the far-right political party that existed in Germany between 1920 and 1945, and rose to power in the 1930s under Adolf Hitler. The party was created to draw workers away from communism, and initially campaigned on an anti-capitalist, anti-bourgeois (middle class), and nationalist platform, but under Hitler the focus shifted to anti-Semitism and anti-Marxism.

Neoliberalism: also known as free market capitalism, this is a form of capitalism involving little state intervention. Neoliberalism assumes that markets can regulate themselves, and that individuals or companies operating within them require minimal rules or oversight.

The New Yorker: a US magazine of essays, satire, fiction, commentary, comics, and poetry established in 1925 and published today by Condé Nast. *The New Yorker* is considered something of an institution: Hannah Arendt's 1968 essay on Walter Benjamin in the magazine would have thus made him a household name in intellectual circles.

"The Painter of Modern Life" (1863): a famous essay by the French poet Charles Baudelaire, in which he calls for artists to change their techniques in order to more fully convey the modern urban experience. Benjamin used the essay in his own writings on nineteenth-century Paris.

Paris shopping arcades: a series of glass-covered streets erected in the center of Paris at the beginning of the nineteenth century to cater to the new middle classes. They were rendered obsolete by advent of department stores in the latter half of the nineteenth century.

Paris Uprisings of May 1968: also known as May '68, these events began as a series of student strikes in the city's high schools and university, and were the culmination of several months of student protest against the endemic elitism in the country's education system.

Political aesthetics: the study of the relationship between art and politics—how political ideas are expressed in art, as well as how political movements adopt artistic strategies, or enlist artists, to promote their particular ideology. "The Work of Art" is an example of political aesthetics, which Benjamin himself helped pioneer.

Psychoanalysis: a system of thought that seeks to treat mental disorders by examining the relationship between conscious behavior and unconscious thoughts, impulses, and desires. Psychoanalysis had an enormous influence on many of the art and literary movements of Benjamin's day, particularly surrealism. Benjamin himself applies its ideas in his writings on modern art, literature, and nineteenth-century Paris.

Radical: departing from tradition; breaking with the past; seeking to change the status quo; fundamentally altering something. Benjamin's work espouses radical views, and he is interested in how reproducibility might aid in opposing fascism and radically changing society.

Reactionary: right-wing, conservative, or otherwise opposed to social reform or progress. Benjamin's work seeks to combat fascism's reactionary tendencies, which involved the celebration of a largely mythical past, and to instead mobilize cinema and photography to effect positive social change.

Reichstag: a historic building in Berlin (Germany), opened in 1894 and home to the Imperial Diet (parliament) of the German Empire until 1933 when the fascist party set it on fire.

Rhetoric: the art of persuasive speech or writing, which involves exploiting figures of speech and particular images that will resonate with the public. Benjamin was interested in the rhetoric used by the fascist part in the late 1930s to mobilize public opinion, which he argued adopted many of the ideas used in traditional art criticism. Rhetoric is also part of what Benjamin sees as the aestheticization of politics in the modern era.

Socialism: an economic model that involves the communal ownership of the means of production, distribution, and exchange. Within Marxist theory, socialism is a transitional state between the overthrowing of capitalism and the ideal, which is communism.

Soviet Union: A single-party Marxist-Leninist state comprising fifteen socialist republics in Eastern Europe that existed between 1922 and 1991.

Standstill: a term used by the playwright Bertolt Brecht to denote a specific moment during a theatrical performance when the action stops, thus jolting the audience into remembering that this is a performance, as well as allowing them time to critique what is happening. Benjamin wrote extensively about this concept, which also informs his ideas about spectatorship in the age of mechanical reproduction.

Surrealism: a countercultural artistic movement born in early-twentieth-century Paris as a reaction to consumer culture and to the commercialization of art. The movement sought to challenge boundaries between reality and unreality, the external world and the unconscious mind, and even life and art. These ideas were influenced by Romanticism.

Technique: in the arts, this refers to the manner in which an artwork (painting, novel, sculpture, etc.) is executed, e.g. broad brushstrokes, or long sentences, or rough edges. This contrasts with the *content*, which instead refers to what the artwork actually communicates.

Technological reproduction: the copying of an artwork through technological means (e.g. photography), rather than manual replication (e.g. replicating a painting by painting another one).

"Theses on the Philosophy of History" (1940): a famous essay by Benjamin that critiques historicism and the view of the past as a "a chain of events" marking progress.

Thesis: a statement put forward in an essay, speech, or other written/verbal work that the work then seeks to demonstrate. In Benjamin's work, the thesis is part of a "dialectical" approach, which seeks to get at the truth by working out the differences between two opposing views.

Totalitarianism: a centralized system of government that requires citizens to be completely subservient to the state. While authoritarianism involves the monopoly of power by an individual or small group, totalitarianism involves the individual/group's efforts to control *all* aspects of social life, and to use the population itself to attain its aims.

"Traditional and Critical Theory" (1937): an essay by Frankfurt School leader Max Horkheimer that pits the theoretical approach usually found in the natural sciences (involving observation and explanation) against what he calls "critical theory," which instead seeks to challenge the status quo, and in particular the capitalist order. Walter Benjamin's work can be seen to follow this latter approach.

Urbanization: refers to the development of rural areas into cities as well as the transformative effects of the growth and expansion of cities. Much of Benjamin's work examines the experience of city living under capitalism, and how the city of Paris in particular functioned as the symbolic center of European capitalism during the nineteenth century.

User-generated content: a term used to refer to media content authored by the audiences or "users" of a media platform or publication rather than by professional writers. The term is usually used in reference to online media—particularly social media—but also applies to earlier forms, such as the "letter to the editor" format that emerged in newspapers and magazines around 1900.

Vietnam War (1955–75): a Cold War-era★ conflict fought in Laos, Cambodia, and Vietnam from 1955 to 1975 between the communist regime of North Vietnam and the capitalist South Vietnam. European and US protests against the war from the mid-1960s until its end fed into a broader anti-establishment mood involving the questioning of tradition and authority. It was in this context that the first English-language edition of Benjamin's text appeared.

Ways of Seeing: a 1972 BBC television series hosted by cultural critic John Berger and adapted by Berger in 1973 into a book of the same name. Both the series and the book were designed to criticize traditional art history and drew heavily on Walter Benjamin's essay to do so.

West Germany: also known as the Federal Republic of Germany (FRG) was the part of Germany that was aligned with other capitalist countries during the Cold War,★ from its creation on May 23, 1949 to the fall of the Berlin Wall on October 3, 1990. The Berlin Wall separated West Germany from communist East Germany. The wall divided Berlin itself, so that part of the city belonged to West Germany and the other part to East Germany.

Western Marxism: a philosophy followed in Western and Central Europe by theorists who apply Marx's ideas, and who are distinct from Marxist philosophers working within the Soviet Union. The term itself was coined in the 1950s by the French philosopher Maurice Merleau-Ponty, and has been retroactively applied to define the work of Benjamin and others associated with the Frankfurt School.

World War I (1914–1918): a global war fought between the Allies (led by Russia, France, Italy, the United States, and the UK), and the Central Powers (led by Germany and Austria–Hungary). Germany lost the war and its economy was subsequently ravaged, leading to mass poverty that then paved the way for the rise of fascism.

World War II (1939–1945): a global war fought between the Allies (led by the Soviet Union, the UK, and the US) and the Axis Powers (led by Germany, Italy, and Japan), which resulted in the genocide of several million Jews across Europe.

PEOPLE MENTIONED IN THE TEXT

Theodor W. Adorno (1903–69) was a seminal German philosopher, sociologist and Marxist critic best known for co-authoring *Dialectic of Enlightenment: Philosophical Fragments* with Max Horkheimer. He was a leader of the Institute for Social Research in Frankfurt and a friend of Walter Benjamin.

Hannah Arendt (1906–75) was a Jewish German-American writer and political theorist best known for her writings on Nazism, totalitarianism, and violence. She was the editor of the first English translation of *Schriften* (the collection of essays by Benjamin in which "The Work of Art in the Age of Mechanical Reproduction" was first published).

Eugène Atget (1857–1927) was a French pioneer of documentary photography best known for his efforts to photograph the streets and architecture of Paris before they were demolished, redeveloped, or modernized. Benjamin cites these photographs as evidence of the political nature of modern art.

Georges Bataille (1897–1962) was a French writer and intellectual involved in the French avant-garde, and a librarian at the central library in Paris when Hitler rose to power. Walter Benjamin left his manuscripts with Bataille when he fled France.

Charles Baudelaire (1821–67) was a French essayist, poet and art critic best known for his writings about modernity and the city. His work profoundly influenced Walter Benjamin, who wrote several essays on him as well as translating his poetry.

John Berger (1926–2017) was an English writer, artist, critic, and political activist. He was the author of many books of art criticism as well as novels, poetry, and documentary essays, of which his most famous, *Ways of Seeing*, is based on "The Work of Art."

Bertolt Brecht (1898–1956) was a German Marxist playwright, poet, and theatre director, and a close friend of Walter Benjamin's. He is best known for his radical approach to narrative, which is often discussed in relation to the European avant-garde, and his explicit criticisms of capitalism, middle class values, and Nazi Germany.

Susan Buck-Morss is an American cultural historian and philosopher, and a leading Walter Benjamin scholar best known for *The Origin of Negative Dialectics: Theodor W. Adorno, Walter Benjamin, and the Frankfurt Institute* (1977) and *The Dialectics of Seeing. Walter Benjamin and the Arcades Project* (1989). She is an ardent critic of the de-politicization of Benjamin's work by art and literature scholars in the US.

George Bush (b. 1924) is a US Republican politician and served as the 41st president of the USA from 1989 to 1993.

Terry Eagleton (b. 1943) is a British Marxist literary critic and Distinguished Professor at Lancaster University who studied under the Marxist literary critic Raymond Williams and is best known for his writings on literary theory and Marxist literary studies. Eagleton published a book on Benjamin in 1981 that emphasized his radicalism.

Howard Eiland is a professor of literature at Harvard University, and a leading translator and editor of several volumes of Walter Benjamin's work, including the first English language edition of the *Arcades Project*. Eiland has also co-written a biography of Benjamin, titled *Walter Benjamin: A Critical Life*.

Friedrich Engels (1820–95) was a German philosopher and close colleague of Karl Marx (1818–1883), best known for co-authoring the *Communist Manifesto* (1848). Engels and Marx's work greatly influenced Benjamin.

Jonathan Franzen (b. 1959) is an American novelist best known for his award-winning novel, *The Corrections* (2001). The protagonist's sale of all of his critical theory books, including Walter Benjamin's, in order to fund an expensive romantic date, has been interpreted as parodying the unpopularity of critical theory in the US during the 1990s, a decade of unusual prosperity.

Erich Fromm (1900–80) was a German philosopher, psychologist, and sociologist associated with the Frankfurt School. He is best known for his first book, *Escape from Freedom* (1941), which is considered to be the first work of political psychology, and his later book, *The Art of Loving* (1956).

Adolf Hitler (1889–1945) was the Führer (leader) of Germany from 1934 to 1945 and was responsible for the persecution and genocide of several million Jews. Benjamin was forced to live in exile in March 1933 due to the Nazis' requisition of German citizenship from German Jews, and allegedly committed suicide while attempting to escape from occupied France into Spain.

Max Horkheimer (1895–1973) was a seminal leftist German Jewish sociologist and philosopher and a leader of the "Frankfurt School" best known for his collaborative authorship, with Theodor Adorno, of *Dialectic of Enlightenment: Philosophical Fragments* (1947). Together with Adorno, Horkheimer also published the first version of Benjamin's essay, and funded some of his other research.

Siegfried Kracauer (1889–1966) was a German Jewish cultural critic, sociologist, film theorist and journalist best known for the essays collected in *The Mass Ornament* (1963). He was a friend of Benjamin's, but disagreed with Benjamin's positive assessment of mass culture, arguing that its distracting qualities served to prevent the masses from revolting.

Esther Leslie (b. 1964) is a leading scholar of Walter Benjamin's work, and a professor of political aesthetics at Birkbeck College, University of London. Leslie has published a number of books on Benjamin that focus on the political dimension of his writings, and is part of a broader effort to re-politicize his work.

Georg Lukács (1885–1971) was a Hungarian philosopher and literary critic who later renounced his early work in the alternative Western Marxist tradition that he partly inaugurated with his seminal text *History and Class Consciousness: Studies in Marxist Dialectics*.

Herbert Marcuse (1898–1979) was a Jewish German-American philosopher and Marxist theorist closely associated with the Frankfurt School and known for his involvement in the student movements of the 1960s in France, Germany, and the US. He escaped the Nazis in 1933 and gained US citizenship in 1940.

Karl Marx (1818–83) was a German political philosopher and economist whose analysis of class relations under capitalism and articulation of a more egalitarian system provided the basis for communism. He wrote *The Communist Manifesto* (1848) with Friedrich Engels★ (1820–95); he articulated his full theory of production and class relations in *Das Kapital* (1867–1894).

Maurice Merleau-Ponty (1908–61) was a French phenomenological philosopher and writer, and the only major philosopher of his time to incorporate descriptive psychology in his work. Ponty was strongly influenced by Marxist thought, and is said to have coined the term "Western Marxism."

Jay Parini (b. 1948) is an American academic and writer best known for his works of criticism, poetry, and biographical novels. In 1997, Parini published a biographical novel about Walter Benjamin's escape from France in 1940, titled *Benjamin's Crossing.*

Dora Sophie Pollak (1890–1964) was Walter Benjamin's wife between 1918 and 1928, with whom he had a troubled marriage marked by financial insecurity and long periods of separation resulting from Benjamin's writing commitments abroad. The couple had one son, Stefan.

Alois Riegl (1858–1905) was an Austrian art historian and theorist who was a key figure in the emergence of art history as a distinctive discipline, and is best known for *Problems of Style* (1893) and *Late Roman Art Industry* (1905). Benjamin was influenced by Riegl's view that artworks should be understood in relation to the economic context in which they were produced.

Ronald Reagan (1911–2004) was a US film actor turned Republican politician who served as the 40th president of the USA from 1981 to 1989.

Gershom Scholem (1897–1982) was a German-born Israeli historian, philosopher and Jewish mystic, regarded today as one of the founders of the academic study of Kabbalah.

Susan Sontag (1933–2004) was a Jewish American writer and political activist best known for her books, *On Photography* (1977), *Illness as Metaphor* (1978), and *AIDS and Its Metaphors* (1988), and collections of essays, such as *Under the Sign of Saturn* (1980), which took its title from Sontag's essay on Walter Benjamin, based on an expression he used to describe himself.

Donald Trump (b. 1946) is a real estate mogul, television celebrity, and the 45th president of the US as of January 2017. Both his deft use of the media during his presidential campaign and his nationalist rhetoric have been repeatedly likened to those of the fascist leaders of the 1930s.

Paul Valéry (1871–1945) was a French poet and essayist best known for his involvement with the French symbolist movement in poetry. Walter Benjamin quotes his essay on technology, "The Conquest of Ubiquity" (1928) in "The Work of Art."

Virginia Woolf (1882–1941) is considered to be among the most influential and important writers of the twentieth century. Woolf is best known for her novel *Mrs Dalloway* (1925) and her essay "A Room of One's Own" (1929). Because of Woolf's extensive engagement with technology in her writing, literary scholars often use Benjamin's ideas in their analyses of her work.

Gustav Wyneken (1875–1964) was a German educational reformer known for his influential, if controversial, views. His idea that youth groups should be led by older members rather than by adults influenced the German Youth Movement (youth groups focused on outdoor activities). His justification of erotic love between teachers and pupils, however, resulted in his conviction, in 1921, for committing vice with minors. Walter Benjamin attended Wyneken's boarding school between 1905 and 1907 and was highly influenced by his political ideas.

WORKS CITED

WORKS CITED

Adorno, Theodor W. "A Portrait of Walter Benjamin." *Prisms*. Translated by Samuel and Shierry Weber. Cambridge, MA: MIT, 1988. 227–42.

— "The Essay as Form." In *Notes to Literature: Volume One*. Translated by Shierry Weber Nicholsen. New York: Columbia University Press, 1991. 3–23.

Adorno, Theodor W., and Walter Benjamin. *The Complete Correspondence:1928–40*. Translated by Nicholas Walker. Cambridge: Polity, 1999.

Andrejevic, Mark. "The *Jouissance* of Trump." *Television and New Media* 17, no. 7 (2016): 651–55.

Benjamin, Walter. *The Arcades Project.* Edited and translated by Howard Eiland and Kevin McLaughlin. Cambridge, MA: Belknap/Harvard University Press, 1999.

— "The Author as Producer." In *Understanding Brecht*. Translated by Anna Bostock. London: Verso, 2003. 85–103.

— "Dream Kitsch: Gloss on Surrealism" (1925). In *The Work of Art in the Age of its Technical Reproducibility and Other Writings.* Edited by Michael W. Jennings et al. Translated by Edmund Jephcott, Rodney Livingstone, Howard Eiland et al. Cambridge, MA: Belknap/Harvard University Press, 2008. 236–39.

— *Schriften.* Frankfurt am Main: Suhrkamp Verlag, 1955.

— "A Small History of Photography." In *One-Way Street and Other Writings*. Translated by Edmund Jephcott and Kingsley Shorter. London: Verso, 1999. 240–57.

— "The Storyteller." In *Illuminations.* Translated by Harry Zohn. London: Fontana, 1982. 83–109.

— "The Work of Art in the Age of Mechanical Reproduction," in *Illuminations,* ed. Hannah Arendt. London: Pimlico, 1999.

— "Surrealism" (1929). In *One-Way Street and Other Writings.* Translated by J. A. Underwood and edited by Amit Chaudhuri. London: Penguin, 2009. 143–60.

— "Theses on the Philosophy of History." In *Illuminations*. Translated by Harry Zohn. London: Fontana, 1982. 255–66.

Understanding Brecht. Translated by Anna Bostock. London: Verso, 1998.

— "The Work of Art in the Age of Mechanical Reproduction." In *One-Way Street and Other Writings.* Edited by Amit Chaudhuri and translated by J. A. Underwood. London and New York: Penguin, 2008. 228–59.

— "The Work of Art in the Age of Its Technological Reproducibility." In *The Work of Art in the Age of Its Technological Reproducibility and Other Writings on Media*. Edited by Michael W. Jennings, Brigid Doherty, Thomas Y. Levin. Cambridge, MA: Belknap/Harvard University Press, 2008. 19–55.

Berger, John. *Ways of Seeing.* London: Penguin, 1977.

Berkowitz, Roger, and Taun N. Toay, eds. *The Intellectual Origins of the Global Financial Crisis.* New York: Fordham University Press, 2013.

Binnet, Alexander. "Donald Trump and the Aesthetics of Fascism: What a 20th-century Marxist art critic can teach us about a very 21st-century candidate." *In These Times* (January 28, 2016). Accessed June 28, 2017. http://inthesetimes. com/article/18807/donald-trump-and-the-aesthetics-of-fascism.

Brownstein, Ronald. "Trump's rhetoric of white nostalgia." *The Atlantic* (June 2, 2016). Accessed June 30, 2017. https://www.theatlantic.com/politics/archive/2016/06/trumps-rhetoric-of-white-nostalgia/485192/.

Buck-Morss, Susan. "Revolutionary Time: The Vanguard and the Avant-Garde." In *Benjamin Studies, Studien 1.* Edited by Helga Geyer Ryan. Amsterdam: Rodopi, 2002.

Caughie, Pamela. *Virginia Woolf in the Age of Mechanical Reproduction.* London: Routledge, 2000.

Clarke, John. "Cultural Studies: a British inheritance." In *New Times and Old Enemies: Essays on Cultural Studies and America.* New York: HarperCollins, 1991.

Denby, David. "The Plot Against America: Trump's Rhetoric." *New Yorker* (Dec. 15, 2015). Accessed June 30, 2017. http://www.newyorker.com/culture/cultural-comment/plot-america-donald-trumps-rhetoric.

Dumm, Thomas. "Degraded fascism, nihilism, and Donald Trump." *Contemporary Condition* (September 2015). Accessed June 28, 2017. http://contemporarycondition.blogspot.co.uk/2015/09/degraded-fascism-nihilism-and-donald.html.

Duttlinger, Caroline. "Between Contemplation and Distraction: Configurations of Attention in Walter Benjamin." *German Studies Review* 30, no. 1 (February 2007): 33–54.

Eagleton, Terry. *Walter Benjamin; or, Towards a Revolutionary Criticism.* London: Verso, 1981.

Eiland, Howard, and Michael W. Jennings. *Walter Benjamin: A Critical Life.* Cambridge, MA: Belknap/Harvard University Press, 2013.

Feigel, Lara. *Literature, Cinema, and Politics 1930–1945: Reading Between the Frames.* Edinburgh University Press, 2010.

Foster, Peter. "The rise of the far-right in Europe is not a false alarm." *Telegraph* (May 19, 2016). Accessed June 30, 2017. http://www.telegraph.co.uk/news/2016/05/19/the-rise-of-the-far-right-in-europe-is-not-a-false-alarm/

Franzen, Jonathan. *The Corrections.* London: Fourth Estate, 2001.

Goebel, Rolf. "Introduction: Benjamin's Actuality." In *A Companion to the Works of Walter Benjamin.* Edited by Rolf Goebel. London: Camden House, 2009. 1–22.

Goldstein, Donna M., and Kira Hall. "Postelection surrealism and nostalgic racism in the hands of Donald Trump." *HAU: Journal of Ethnographic Theory* 7, no. 1 (2017). http://dx.doi.org/10.14318/hau7.1.026.

Greenberg, Udi E. "The Politics of the Walter Benjamin Industry." *Theory, Culture & Society* 25, no. 3 (2008): 53–68. Accessed June 28, 2017. DOI: 10.1177/0263276408090657.

Gubster, Mike. *Time's Visible Surface: Alois Riegl and the Discourse on History and Temporality in Fin-de-Siécle Vienna.* Detroit, MI: Wayne State University Press, 2006.

Horkheimer, Max. "Traditional and Critical Theory" (1937). In *Selected Essays.* London and New York: Continuum, 1982. 188–244.

Jeffries, Stuart. "Why a forgotten 1930s critique of capitalism is back in fashion." *Guardian* (September 9, 2016). Accessed June 25, 2017. https://www.theguardian.com/books/2016/sep/09/marxist-critique-capitalism-frankfurt-school-cultural-apocalypse.

— *Grand Hotel Abyss: The Lives of the Frankfurt School.* London: Verso, 2016.

Jones, Oliver. *Donald Trump: The Rhetoric.* London: Eyeware Publishing, 2016.

Kang, Jaeho. *Walter Benjamin and the Media: The Spectacle of Modernity.* Cambridge: Polity Press, 2014.

Leith, Sam. "Trump's rhetoric: a triumph of inarticulacy." *Guardian* (January 13, 2017). Accessed June 30, 2017. https://www.theguardian.com/us-news/2017/jan/13/donald-trumps-rhetoric-how-being-inarticulate-is-seen-as-authentic.

Leslie, Esther. *Walter Benjamin: Overpowering Conformism.* London: Reaktion, 2000.

— *Walter Benjamin.* London: Reaktion, 2007.

"Revolutionary potential and Walter Benjamin: A postwar reception history." In *Critical Companion to Contemporary Marxism.* Edited by Gregory Elliot and Jacques Bidet. Leiden: Brill, 2007. 549–66.

— *Hollywood Flatlands, Critical Theory and the Avant-Garde.* London: Verso, 2002.

Levin, T. Y. "Walter Benjamin and the Theory of Art History." *October* 47 (Winter 1988): 77–83.

Lukács, Georg. *History and Class Consciousness: Studies in Marxist Dialectics.* London: Merlin, 1968 (1923).

Mardell, Mark. "Fascism, the 1930s, and the 21st century." *BBC News* (December 20, 2016). Accessed June 30, 2017. http://www.bbc.co.uk/news/uk-politics-38317787.

Marinetti, Tommaso. "Futurist Manifesto" (1908). In *Theories of Modern Art: A Source Book by Artists and Critics.* Edited by Herschel B. Chipp. Berkeley, CA: University of California Press, 1996 (1968). 285–287.

Marx, Karl. "The fetishism of commodities and the secret thereof." *Capital: Unabridged edition.* Edited by David McLellan. Oxford: Oxford University Press, 2008 (1867). 42–50.

McChesney, Robert W. "Whatever happened to cultural studies?" In *American Cultural Studies.* Edited by Catherine A. Warren and Mary Douglas Vavrus. Chicago: University of Illinois Press, 2002. 76–93.

McDougall, James. "No, this isn't the 1930s—but yes, this is fascism." *The Conversation* (November 16, 2016). Accessed June 30, 2017. https://theconversation.com/no-this-isnt-the-1930s-but-yes-this-is-fascism-68867.

McRobbie, Angela. "The *Passagenwerk* and the place of Walter Benjamin in cultural studies. *Cultural Studies* 6, no. 2 (1992): 147–69. Reprinted in: *The Cultural Studies Reader.* Edited by Simon During. London: Routledge, 1999. 77–96.

Meissner, Miriam. *Narrating the Global Financial Crisis: Urban Imaginaries and the Politics of Myth.* New York and Basingstoke: Palgrave, 2017.

Mirowski, Philip. *Never Let a Serious Crisis Go to Waste: How Neoliberalism Survived the Financial Meltdown.* London: Verso, 2013.

Nelson, Cary. "Always Already Cultural Studies." In *English Studies/Cultural Studies: Institutionalizing Dissent.* Edited by Isaiah Smithson and Nancy Ruff. Chicago: University of Illinois Press, 1994. 191–206.

Ortile, Matt. "11 Wonderful Illuminating Quotes from Walter Benjamin: Get ready for some *Illuminations* in Honor of His 122nd Birthday Today!" *Buzzfeed* (July 15, 2014). Accessed June 30, 2017.

https://www.buzzfeed.com/mattortile/work-of-art-in-the-age-of-social-discovery?utm_term=.vb8mqkAAj#.shK5pgyyD.

Palmer, John. "The rise of the far right parties across Europe is a chilling echo of the 1930s." *Guardian* (November 15, 2013). Accessed June 30, 2017. https://www.theguardian.com/commentisfree/2013/nov/15/far-right-threat-europe-integration.

Penney, Joel. *Citizen Marketer: Promoting Political Opinion in the Social Media Age* (Oxford: Oxford University Press, 2017), 113.

Pusca, Anca, ed. *Walter Benjamin and the Aesthetics of Change.* New York and Basingstoke: Palgrave Macmillan, 2010.

Robinson, Andrew. "Walter Benjamin and Critical Theory." *Ceasefire* (April 4, 2013). Accessed June 27, 2017. https://ceasefiremagazine.co.uk/in-theory-benjamin-1/.

Roos, Jeremy. "Trump's victory speaks to a crumbling liberal order." *Road* (November 9, 2016). Accessed June 27, 2017. https://roarmag.org/essays/trump-victory-legitimation-crisis-capitalism/.

Ross, Alex. "The Frankfurt School knew Trump was Coming." *New Yorker* (December 5, 2016). Accessed June 27, 2017. http://www.newyorker.com/culture/cultural-comment/the-frankfurt-school-knew-trump-was-coming.

Schiwy, Freya, and Alessandro Fornazzari, eds. *Digital Media, Cultural Production and Speculative Capitalism.* London: Routledge, 2013.

Shepherd, Laura J., and Caitlin Hamilton, eds. *Understanding Popular Culture and World Politics in the Digital Age.* London: Routledge, 2016.

Sontag, Susan. "The Decay of Cinema." *New York Times* (February 25, 1996). Accessed June 28, 2017. http://www.nytimes.com/books/00/03/12/specials/sontag-cinema.html.

Valéry, Paul. "The Conquest of Ubiquity" (1928). In *Aesthetics*. Translated by Ralph Manheim. New York: Pantheon Books, 1964.

Vassiliou, Konstantinos. "The Aura of Art After the Advent of the Digital." In *Walter Benjamin and the Aesthetics of Change.* Edited by Anca Pusca. New York and Basingstoke: Palgrave Macmillan, 2010. 158–170.

Whyman, Tom. "Which Philosophy Can Best Explain 2016?" *Vice* (December 15, 2016). Accessed June 28, 2017. https://www.vice.com/en_uk/article/z4ngy4/which-philosophy-can-help-us-understand-2016.

Wizislda, Erdmut. *Walter Benjamin and Bertolt Brecht: The Story of a Friendship.* Translated by Christine Shuttleworth. New Haven: Yale University Press, 2009.

Wolff, Janet. "Memoirs and Micrologies: Walter Benjamin, feminism, and cultural analysis." In *Walter Benjamin: Critical Interventions in Cultural Theory. Vol III: Appropriations*. Edited by Peter Osborne. London: Routledge, 2005. 319–33.

THE MACAT LIBRARY
BY DISCIPLINE

The Macat Library By Discipline

AFRICANA STUDIES

Chinua Achebe's *An Image of Africa: Racism in Conrad's Heart of Darkness*
W. E. B. Du Bois's *The Souls of Black Folk*
Zora Neale Huston's *Characteristics of Negro Expression*
Martin Luther King Jr's *Why We Can't Wait*
Toni Morrison's *Playing in the Dark: Whiteness in the American Literary Imagination*

ANTHROPOLOGY

Arjun Appadurai's *Modernity at Large: Cultural Dimensions of Globalisation*
Philippe Ariès's *Centuries of Childhood*
Franz Boas's *Race, Language and Culture*
Kim Chan & Renée Mauborgne's *Blue Ocean Strategy*
Jared Diamond's *Guns, Germs & Steel: the Fate of Human Societies*
Jared Diamond's *Collapse: How Societies Choose to Fail or Survive*
E. E. Evans-Pritchard's *Witchcraft, Oracles and Magic Among the Azande*
James Ferguson's *The Anti-Politics Machine*
Clifford Geertz's *The Interpretation of Cultures*
David Graeber's *Debt: the First 5000 Years*
Karen Ho's *Liquidated: An Ethnography of Wall Street*
Geert Hofstede's *Culture's Consequences: Comparing Values, Behaviors, Institutes and Organizations across Nations*
Claude Lévi-Strauss's *Structural Anthropology*
Jay Macleod's *Ain't No Makin' It: Aspirations and Attainment in a Low-Income Neighborhood*
Saba Mahmood's *The Politics of Piety: The Islamic Revival and the Feminist Subject*
Marcel Mauss's *The Gift*

BUSINESS

Jean Lave & Etienne Wenger's *Situated Learning*
Theodore Levitt's *Marketing Myopia*
Burton G. Malkiel's *A Random Walk Down Wall Street*
Douglas McGregor's *The Human Side of Enterprise*
Michael Porter's *Competitive Strategy: Creating and Sustaining Superior Performance*
John Kotter's *Leading Change*
C. K. Prahalad & Gary Hamel's *The Core Competence of the Corporation*

CRIMINOLOGY

Michelle Alexander's *The New Jim Crow: Mass Incarceration in the Age of Colorblindness*
Michael R. Gottfredson & Travis Hirschi's *A General Theory of Crime*
Richard Herrnstein & Charles A. Murray's *The Bell Curve: Intelligence and Class Structure in American Life*
Elizabeth Loftus's *Eyewitness Testimony*
Jay Macleod's *Ain't No Makin' It: Aspirations and Attainment in a Low-Income Neighborhood*
Philip Zimbardo's *The Lucifer Effect*

ECONOMICS

Janet Abu-Lughod's *Before European Hegemony*
Ha-Joon Chang's *Kicking Away the Ladder*
David Brion Davis's *The Problem of Slavery in the Age of Revolution*
Milton Friedman's *The Role of Monetary Policy*
Milton Friedman's *Capitalism and Freedom*
David Graeber's *Debt: the First 5000 Years*
Friedrich Hayek's *The Road to Serfdom*
Karen Ho's *Liquidated: An Ethnography of Wall Street*

John Maynard Keynes's *The General Theory of Employment, Interest and Money*
Charles P. Kindleberger's *Manias, Panics and Crashes*
Robert Lucas's *Why Doesn't Capital Flow from Rich to Poor Countries?*
Burton G. Malkiel's *A Random Walk Down Wall Street*
Thomas Robert Malthus's *An Essay on the Principle of Population*
Karl Marx's *Capital*
Thomas Piketty's *Capital in the Twenty-First Century*
Amartya Sen's *Development as Freedom*
Adam Smith's *The Wealth of Nations*
Nassim Nicholas Taleb's *The Black Swan: The Impact of the Highly Improbable*
Amos Tversky's & Daniel Kahneman's *Judgment under Uncertainty: Heuristics and Biases*
Mahbub Ul Haq's *Reflections on Human Development*
Max Weber's *The Protestant Ethic and the Spirit of Capitalism*

FEMINISM AND GENDER STUDIES

Judith Butler's *Gender Trouble*
Simone De Beauvoir's *The Second Sex*
Michel Foucault's *History of Sexuality*
Betty Friedan's *The Feminine Mystique*
Saba Mahmood's *The Politics of Piety: The Islamic Revival and the Feminist Subject*
Joan Wallach Scott's *Gender and the Politics of History*
Mary Wollstonecraft's *A Vindication of the Rights of Women*
Virginia Woolf's *A Room of One's Own*

GEOGRAPHY

The Brundtland Report's *Our Common Future*
Rachel Carson's *Silent Spring*
Charles Darwin's *On the Origin of Species*
James Ferguson's *The Anti-Politics Machine*
Jane Jacobs's *The Death and Life of Great American Cities*
James Lovelock's *Gaia: A New Look at Life on Earth*
Amartya Sen's *Development as Freedom*
Mathis Wackernagel & William Rees's *Our Ecological Footprint*

HISTORY

Janet Abu-Lughod's *Before European Hegemony*
Benedict Anderson's *Imagined Communities*
Bernard Bailyn's *The Ideological Origins of the American Revolution*
Hanna Batatu's *The Old Social Classes And The Revolutionary Movements Of Iraq*
Christopher Browning's *Ordinary Men: Reserve Police Batallion 101 and the Final Solution in Poland*
Edmund Burke's *Reflections on the Revolution in France*
William Cronon's *Nature's Metropolis: Chicago And The Great West*
Alfred W. Crosby's *The Columbian Exchange*
Hamid Dabashi's *Iran: A People Interrupted*
David Brion Davis's *The Problem of Slavery in the Age of Revolution*
Nathalie Zemon Davis's *The Return of Martin Guerre*
Jared Diamond's *Guns, Germs & Steel: the Fate of Human Societies*
Frank Dikotter's *Mao's Great Famine*
John W Dower's *War Without Mercy: Race And Power In The Pacific War*
W. E. B. Du Bois's *The Souls of Black Folk*
Richard J. Evans's *In Defence of History*
Lucien Febvre's *The Problem of Unbelief in the 16th Century*
Sheila Fitzpatrick's *Everyday Stalinism*

The Macat Library By Discipline

Eric Foner's *Reconstruction: America's Unfinished Revolution, 1863-1877*
Michel Foucault's *Discipline and Punish*
Michel Foucault's *History of Sexuality*
Francis Fukuyama's *The End of History and the Last Man*
John Lewis Gaddis's *We Now Know: Rethinking Cold War History*
Ernest Gellner's *Nations and Nationalism*
Eugene Genovese's *Roll, Jordan, Roll: The World the Slaves Made*
Carlo Ginzburg's *The Night Battles*
Daniel Goldhagen's *Hitler's Willing Executioners*
Jack Goldstone's *Revolution and Rebellion in the Early Modern World*
Antonio Gramsci's *The Prison Notebooks*
Alexander Hamilton, John Jay & James Madison's *The Federalist Papers*
Christopher Hill's *The World Turned Upside Down*
Carole Hillenbrand's *The Crusades: Islamic Perspectives*
Thomas Hobbes's *Leviathan*
Eric Hobsbawm's *The Age Of Revolution*
John A. Hobson's *Imperialism: A Study*
Albert Hourani's *History of the Arab Peoples*
Samuel P. Huntington's *The Clash of Civilizations and the Remaking of World Order*
C. L. R. James's *The Black Jacobins*
Tony Judt's *Postwar: A History of Europe Since 1945*
Ernst Kantorowicz's *The King's Two Bodies: A Study in Medieval Political Theology*
Paul Kennedy's *The Rise and Fall of the Great Powers*
Ian Kershaw's *The "Hitler Myth": Image and Reality in the Third Reich*
John Maynard Keynes's *The General Theory of Employment, Interest and Money*
Charles P. Kindleberger's *Manias, Panics and Crashes*
Martin Luther King Jr's *Why We Can't Wait*
Henry Kissinger's *World Order: Reflections on the Character of Nations and the Course of History*
Thomas Kuhn's *The Structure of Scientific Revolutions*
Georges Lefebvre's *The Coming of the French Revolution*
John Locke's *Two Treatises of Government*
Niccolò Machiavelli's *The Prince*
Thomas Robert Malthus's *An Essay on the Principle of Population*
Mahmood Mamdani's *Citizen and Subject: Contemporary Africa And The Legacy Of Late Colonialism*
Karl Marx's *Capital*
Stanley Milgram's *Obedience to Authority*
John Stuart Mill's *On Liberty*
Thomas Paine's *Common Sense*
Thomas Paine's *Rights of Man*
Geoffrey Parker's *Global Crisis: War, Climate Change and Catastrophe in the Seventeenth Century*
Jonathan Riley-Smith's *The First Crusade and the Idea of Crusading*
Jean-Jacques Rousseau's *The Social Contract*
Joan Wallach Scott's *Gender and the Politics of History*
Theda Skocpol's *States and Social Revolutions*
Adam Smith's *The Wealth of Nations*
Timothy Snyder's *Bloodlands: Europe Between Hitler and Stalin*
Sun Tzu's *The Art of War*
Keith Thomas's *Religion and the Decline of Magic*
Thucydides's *The History of the Peloponnesian War*
Frederick Jackson Turner's *The Significance of the Frontier in American History*
Odd Arne Westad's *The Global Cold War: Third World Interventions And The Making Of Our Times*

LITERATURE

Chinua Achebe's *An Image of Africa: Racism in Conrad's Heart of Darkness*
Roland Barthes's *Mythologies*
Homi K. Bhabha's *The Location of Culture*
Judith Butler's *Gender Trouble*
Simone De Beauvoir's *The Second Sex*
Ferdinand De Saussure's *Course in General Linguistics*
T. S. Eliot's *The Sacred Wood: Essays on Poetry and Criticism*
Zora Neale Huston's *Characteristics of Negro Expression*
Toni Morrison's *Playing in the Dark: Whiteness in the American Literary Imagination*
Edward Said's *Orientalism*
Gayatri Chakravorty Spivak's *Can the Subaltern Speak?*
Mary Wollstonecraft's *A Vindication of the Rights of Women*
Virginia Woolf's *A Room of One's Own*

PHILOSOPHY

Elizabeth Anscombe's *Modern Moral Philosophy*
Hannah Arendt's *The Human Condition*
Aristotle's *Metaphysics*
Aristotle's *Nicomachean Ethics*
Edmund Gettier's *Is Justified True Belief Knowledge?*
Georg Wilhelm Friedrich Hegel's *Phenomenology of Spirit*
David Hume's *Dialogues Concerning Natural Religion*
David Hume's *The Enquiry for Human Understanding*
Immanuel Kant's *Religion within the Boundaries of Mere Reason*
Immanuel Kant's *Critique of Pure Reason*
Søren Kierkegaard's *The Sickness Unto Death*
Søren Kierkegaard's *Fear and Trembling*
C. S. Lewis's *The Abolition of Man*
Alasdair MacIntyre's *After Virtue*
Marcus Aurelius's *Meditations*
Friedrich Nietzsche's *On the Genealogy of Morality*
Friedrich Nietzsche's *Beyond Good and Evil*
Plato's *Republic*
Plato's *Symposium*
Jean-Jacques Rousseau's *The Social Contract*
Gilbert Ryle's *The Concept of Mind*
Baruch Spinoza's *Ethics*
Sun Tzu's *The Art of War*
Ludwig Wittgenstein's *Philosophical Investigations*

POLITICS

Benedict Anderson's *Imagined Communities*
Aristotle's *Politics*
Bernard Bailyn's *The Ideological Origins of the American Revolution*
Edmund Burke's *Reflections on the Revolution in France*
John C. Calhoun's *A Disquisition on Government*
Ha-Joon Chang's *Kicking Away the Ladder*
Hamid Dabashi's *Iran: A People Interrupted*
Hamid Dabashi's *Theology of Discontent: The Ideological Foundation of the Islamic Revolution in Iran*
Robert Dahl's *Democracy and its Critics*
Robert Dahl's *Who Governs?*
David Brion Davis's *The Problem of Slavery in the Age of Revolution*

The Macat Library By Discipline

Alexis De Tocqueville's *Democracy in America*
James Ferguson's *The Anti-Politics Machine*
Frank Dikotter's *Mao's Great Famine*
Sheila Fitzpatrick's *Everyday Stalinism*
Eric Foner's *Reconstruction: America's Unfinished Revolution, 1863-1877*
Milton Friedman's *Capitalism and Freedom*
Francis Fukuyama's *The End of History and the Last Man*
John Lewis Gaddis's *We Now Know: Rethinking Cold War History*
Ernest Gellner's *Nations and Nationalism*
David Graeber's *Debt: the First 5000 Years*
Antonio Gramsci's *The Prison Notebooks*
Alexander Hamilton, John Jay & James Madison's *The Federalist Papers*
Friedrich Hayek's *The Road to Serfdom*
Christopher Hill's *The World Turned Upside Down*
Thomas Hobbes's *Leviathan*
John A. Hobson's *Imperialism: A Study*
Samuel P. Huntington's *The Clash of Civilizations and the Remaking of World Order*
Tony Judt's *Postwar: A History of Europe Since 1945*
David C. Kang's *China Rising: Peace, Power and Order in East Asia*
Paul Kennedy's *The Rise and Fall of Great Powers*
Robert Keohane's *After Hegemony*
Martin Luther King Jr.'s *Why We Can't Wait*
Henry Kissinger's *World Order: Reflections on the Character of Nations and the Course of History*
John Locke's *Two Treatises of Government*
Niccolò Machiavelli's *The Prince*
Thomas Robert Malthus's *An Essay on the Principle of Population*
Mahmood Mamdani's *Citizen and Subject: Contemporary Africa And The Legacy Of Late Colonialism*
Karl Marx's *Capital*
John Stuart Mill's *On Liberty*
John Stuart Mill's *Utilitarianism*
Hans Morgenthau's *Politics Among Nations*
Thomas Paine's *Common Sense*
Thomas Paine's *Rights of Man*
Thomas Piketty's *Capital in the Twenty-First Century*
Robert D. Putman's *Bowling Alone*
John Rawls's *Theory of Justice*
Jean-Jacques Rousseau's *The Social Contract*
Theda Skocpol's *States and Social Revolutions*
Adam Smith's *The Wealth of Nations*
Sun Tzu's *The Art of War*
Henry David Thoreau's *Civil Disobedience*
Thucydides's *The History of the Peloponnesian War*
Kenneth Waltz's *Theory of International Politics*
Max Weber's *Politics as a Vocation*
Odd Arne Westad's *The Global Cold War: Third World Interventions And The Making Of Our Times*

POSTCOLONIAL STUDIES

Roland Barthes's *Mythologies*
Frantz Fanon's *Black Skin, White Masks*
Homi K. Bhabha's *The Location of Culture*
Gustavo Gutiérrez's *A Theology of Liberation*
Edward Said's *Orientalism*
Gayatri Chakravorty Spivak's *Can the Subaltern Speak?*

PSYCHOLOGY

Gordon Allport's *The Nature of Prejudice*
Alan Baddeley & Graham Hitch's *Aggression: A Social Learning Analysis*
Albert Bandura's *Aggression: A Social Learning Analysis*
Leon Festinger's *A Theory of Cognitive Dissonance*
Sigmund Freud's *The Interpretation of Dreams*
Betty Friedan's *The Feminine Mystique*
Michael R. Gottfredson & Travis Hirschi's *A General Theory of Crime*
Eric Hoffer's *The True Believer: Thoughts on the Nature of Mass Movements*
William James's *Principles of Psychology*
Elizabeth Loftus's *Eyewitness Testimony*
A. H. Maslow's *A Theory of Human Motivation*
Stanley Milgram's *Obedience to Authority*
Steven Pinker's *The Better Angels of Our Nature*
Oliver Sacks's *The Man Who Mistook His Wife For a Hat*
Richard Thaler & Cass Sunstein's *Nudge: Improving Decisions About Health, Wealth and Happiness*
Amos Tversky's *Judgment under Uncertainty: Heuristics and Biases*
Philip Zimbardo's *The Lucifer Effect*

SCIENCE

Rachel Carson's *Silent Spring*
William Cronon's *Nature's Metropolis: Chicago And The Great West*
Alfred W. Crosby's *The Columbian Exchange*
Charles Darwin's *On the Origin of Species*
Richard Dawkin's *The Selfish Gene*
Thomas Kuhn's *The Structure of Scientific Revolutions*
Geoffrey Parker's *Global Crisis: War, Climate Change and Catastrophe in the Seventeenth Century*
Mathis Wackernagel & William Rees's *Our Ecological Footprint*

SOCIOLOGY

Michelle Alexander's *The New Jim Crow: Mass Incarceration in the Age of Colorblindness*
Gordon Allport's *The Nature of Prejudice*
Albert Bandura's *Aggression: A Social Learning Analysis*
Hanna Batatu's *The Old Social Classes And The Revolutionary Movements Of Iraq*
Ha-Joon Chang's *Kicking Away the Ladder*
W. E. B. Du Bois's *The Souls of Black Folk*
Émile Durkheim's *On Suicide*
Frantz Fanon's *Black Skin, White Masks*
Frantz Fanon's *The Wretched of the Earth*
Eric Foner's *Reconstruction: America's Unfinished Revolution, 1863-1877*
Eugene Genovese's *Roll, Jordan, Roll: The World the Slaves Made*
Jack Goldstone's *Revolution and Rebellion in the Early Modern World*
Antonio Gramsci's *The Prison Notebooks*
Richard Herrnstein & Charles A Murray's *The Bell Curve: Intelligence and Class Structure in American Life*
Eric Hoffer's *The True Believer: Thoughts on the Nature of Mass Movements*
Jane Jacobs's *The Death and Life of Great American Cities*
Robert Lucas's *Why Doesn't Capital Flow from Rich to Poor Countries?*
Jay Macleod's *Ain't No Makin' It: Aspirations and Attainment in a Low Income Neighborhood*
Elaine May's *Homeward Bound: American Families in the Cold War Era*
Douglas McGregor's *The Human Side of Enterprise*
C. Wright Mills's *The Sociological Imagination*

The Macat Library By Discipline

Thomas Piketty's *Capital in the Twenty-First Century*
Robert D. Putman's *Bowling Alone*
David Riesman's *The Lonely Crowd: A Study of the Changing American Character*
Edward Said's *Orientalism*
Joan Wallach Scott's *Gender and the Politics of History*
Theda Skocpol's *States and Social Revolutions*
Max Weber's *The Protestant Ethic and the Spirit of Capitalism*

THEOLOGY

Augustine's *Confessions*
Benedict's *Rule of St Benedict*
Gustavo Gutiérrez's *A Theology of Liberation*
Carole Hillenbrand's *The Crusades: Islamic Perspectives*
David Hume's *Dialogues Concerning Natural Religion*
Immanuel Kant's *Religion within the Boundaries of Mere Reason*
Ernst Kantorowicz's *The King's Two Bodies: A Study in Medieval Political Theology*
Søren Kierkegaard's *The Sickness Unto Death*
C. S. Lewis's *The Abolition of Man*
Saba Mahmood's *The Politics of Piety: The Islamic Revival and the Feminist Subject*
Baruch Spinoza's *Ethics*
Keith Thomas's *Religion and the Decline of Magic*

COMING SOON

Chris Argyris's *The Individual and the Organisation*
Seyla Benhabib's *The Rights of Others*
Walter Benjamin's *The Work Of Art in the Age of Mechanical Reproduction*
John Berger's *Ways of Seeing*
Pierre Bourdieu's *Outline of a Theory of Practice*
Mary Douglas's *Purity and Danger*
Roland Dworkin's *Taking Rights Seriously*
James G. March's *Exploration and Exploitation in Organisational Learning*
Ikujiro Nonaka's *A Dynamic Theory of Organizational Knowledge Creation*
Griselda Pollock's *Vision and Difference*
Amartya Sen's *Inequality Re-Examined*
Susan Sontag's *On Photography*
Yasser Tabbaa's *The Transformation of Islamic Art*
Ludwig von Mises's *Theory of Money and Credit*

Printed in the United States
by Baker & Taylor Publisher Services